Claim!

' ARCHITECTURE

IS THE CHILD OF

NECESSITY AND

THE PARENT OF

GENERAL UTILITY

Sir John Soane. '

All the quotations in this section are
taken from Sir John Soane's lectures in
architecture delivered to the Royal
Academy in 1809 and 1815.

A RUTLAND PRESS BOOK

© Charles McKean 1998.

Published for RIAS Insurance Services Limited
by The Rutland Press
15 Rutland Square
Edinburgh EH1 2BE

ISBN 1-873-190-336

This book was designed and produced by
The Design Foundry (Scotland) Limited
56 Tower Street
Edinburgh EH6 7BN

Foreword

Learning does not have to be a painful process; as with an illness, the pain of dealing with a professional negligence claim can be seen as an opportunity for change and improvement. Whether this occurs or not is a function of the attitude of the practice and the insurance company, and whether practical arrangements are in place for the lessons learnt to be applied in future.

Of all the excellent characteristics of RIAS Insurance Services Ltd, the willingness of the company to assist the learning process must be recognised as one of its major contributions to professional life in Scotland.

The claims feedbacks, published regularly in the monthly *Chartered Architect*, are read avidly, if with a sense of doom. Their punchy style and succinctness are lessons on communication sadly an art the profession as a whole seems not to have mastered, at its continuing peril.

This unique book should be read by architects everywhere: if it is, the profession's health should improve dramatically!

Sebastian Tombs FRIAS RIBA ACIArb
SECRETARY & TREASURER

SECTION ONE: CONTEXT

What happens once a building contract turns sour and a claim has to be made, is as much of a mystery to client as it is to architect. And even after having had to endure a claim process, they may never be fully aware of how they are perceived by others, or the methodology which was followed, or understand the often seemingly incomprehensible basis for settlement. This book seeks to clarify what happens, by reconsidering the case studies extracted from RIAS Insurance Services' claims files which have been published in the RIAS *Chartered Architect* since 1993. It provides the opportunity to examine some of the broader issues that emerge between one claim and the next. The bulk of the book is made up of the assessment from 52 RIASIS files, and a reprinting of 47 of those (five earlier ones were published in summary form in December 1990). The insurers selected these cases from 2165 claims lodged since 1984, of which 1941 have been finalised. However, they represent just under half of all those in which a financial settlement has been made: a ratio of paid settlement to lodged claim of under 10% . No pattern to their selection was disclosed, save that the author might find them interesting.

These are the insurer's files. The primary correspondent is the loss adjuster or the lawyer, with, as necessary, reports from expert witnesses and occasional letters of authority from underwriters. Once the notification is made, we hear no more of the architect, nor of his pleas of (sometimes justifiable) anguished innocence. It is the loss adjuster who hears all that and evaluates it coldly. Although over half went to the stage of a writ or a closed record , all were settled out of court, generally at a sum substantially less than that originally sued for. So the judgements upon which the cases were concluded make neither case law nor precedent; indeed, in many cases, one might question whether the law would have upheld the basis of settlement – had either party the funds or stamina to take it to that extremity.

The priority for the insurer and for most clients is to achieve the best possible settlement. Generally, the insurance company's policy is that of *festina lente*: don't harry the client, but respond immediately once the client acts. Its principal difficulty is to establish the credibility of

'occasionally, claims were settled by attrition'

the architect's case where there is inadequate documentation to support it. The initiative lies with the claimant, who has the duty to specify the claim and justify the alleged loss; and delays are usually attributable to the claimant's failure to undertake this adequately. Speed appears to be less critical for insurer or client than it is for the architect, who may have to carry a claim through several years of renewal, to his emotional and financial disadvantage. It is only once the claim is time-barred, that the insurer can close the file unilaterally. Occasionally the claims were settled by attrition: one lasted six years, and another 12.

The files all follow a comparable format. Notification is received, usually from the architect. Once an identifiable threat is manifest, the insurer appoints a loss adjuster or solicitor to prepare a preliminary report. The preliminary report assesses the allegation and makes a provisional assessment of liability with a suggested reserve (if any). This report requires co-operation from the architect, and his files. Those who are tardy in response or go into denial, damage themselves. Although it is understandable that both parties are likely to feel aggressive in a fractured relationship, the number of architects acting thrawn in the face of threat is astounding. During this initial period, the amount being sued for tends to increase. The client is aware that an insurer is now involved, and much of the residual angst, always present in a building contract which has gone sour, begins to leak out. So other problematic aspects of the commission are tossed in, eventually reaching what may be nicknamed 'the peak' – a vast sum representing extraordinary malfeasance. The remainder of the file – later loss adjusters' reports, expert witness's reports where required, open and closed records for the court – represent the loss adjuster chipping away at that 'peak' until a more reasonable settlement could be excavated from its lower slopes.

The Profession-Insurer Relationship

The prospectus for the establishment of RIAS Insurance Services Ltd in 1984 emphasised the innovations of the new scheme: the involvement of the RIAS, the appointment of a senior member as chairman; wider and improved policy wording – in particular, the provision of cover for innocent non-disclosure (at a time when that was uncommon); local handling of cases by loss adjusters and solicitors in various parts of Scotland; and a provision for reference to senior architects where a dispute existed between the company and the insured. The company and the RIAS together aspired to achieve 70% of the Scottish architectural market within three years and, if that were achieved, to bring stability to the 'annual increases' of premiums which had been so desperate between 1977 and 1984. The company also undertook to assist the RIAS in challenging the law as it related to architects, and to create close links between the insurance company, underwriters, and RIAS Practice Services. Finally, it undertook to focus upon claims' prevention 'including feedback on the results of legal cases'.

A 60% take-up of the market was achieved within the first year, and the optimum target of 70% was exceeded in the following year Since then the percentage of Scottish architects to take up insurance with RIAS Insurance Services Ltd has fluctuated between 74-86%. The premium pattern was even more striking. Premiums continued generally to rise until year three (1987), since which time they have been falling heavily. In 1984, it was customary for a practice to be paying 5-8% (Scotland) or 7-12% (England) of gross fee turnover for professional indemnity insurance cover. By 1993, the average amount that practices in Scotland paid had reduced to c.2.5% of turnover and could be much less. The market in 1998 is slightly softer yet, with practices having only to budget 1.5%-2.5% of gross fee turnover for adequate cover.

It was always the intention of the company to explore whether or not there was a differential claims' pattern between Scotland and England. By 1994, the underwriters were convinced that Scotland's record was indeed better. For many reasons – not least because of the relative shortage of very large, very complicated building projects of which there have been so many in south-east England – the number of large claims has been agreeably small.

The initial links between the insurance company and the Incorporation have persisted. Insurance Committee members have enjoyed direct dialogue with the underwriters who have frequently sponsored Incorporation events such as the annual RIAS Convention, *Prospect* magazine, and the Edinburgh Festival exhibitions. RIAS Insurance Services Ltd supported the establishment of RIAS CPD in 1987, and has contributed to it since; it supported the RIAS representation to the Scottish Law Commission on the reform of liability law, and assisted with the *RIAS Practice Guide*.

In pursuit, however, of sustained feedback to architects and clients, in 1987 RIASIS began the publication of very broad data about the size of claims, and the identification of broad client type. Since then, it has commissioned two major projects. The first was a study of consumer reaction to the company in 1992. Since that coincided with the RIAS Quality Campaign, and the first emergence of RIAS Consultancy, that study included a survey of office practice, job costing and fee tendering. The result was published in 1994 as *Value or Cost*[ ]. Then, in 1993, it began the serial publication of the analysis of specific cases to illuminate the general principles which had been published in earlier years. In 1994, it published a review of its first decade of operation *Professional Indemnity Insurance – the results*[ ], with contributions from solicitors, the company, the RIAS, the Construction Industry Council and the Association of Consultant Architects. The latter stated *'when ACA finally decided to launch its own insurance scheme, we naturally turned to the RIAS scheme as a model'*[ ].

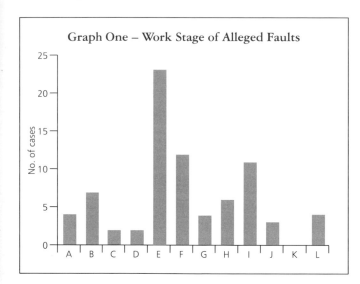

Graph One – Work Stage of Alleged Faults

Claims and the Policy

Around 55% of the claims were received post-completion of the commission. All but one of the balance were received at some stage during construction, mostly towards the final stages. However, the primary alleged fault – i.e. the principal cause of claim – is far more spread throughout all the work stages. Graph One shows a cluster at feasibility (stage B – well, if you must build on someone else's land …), and the greatest concentration – over 50% – at specification, detailed design and contract documentation stages (Stages E, F and G). Claims arising

from the construction process were under half that figure. Secondary faults – that is other weaknesses in the architect's performance sufficient to feature as a factor in the file – occur preponderantly during the contract. It implies that once something is going wrong, remedial action on site may serve only to exacerbate the problem.

No obvious lesson emerges from a study of the building types, save that they are generally in line with Scottish construction over the period (Graph Two) Over 50% of claims related to residential work, followed by commercial work, sports, industrial, and institutional buildings, and speculative developments. The most frequently claiming client is the owner/occupier (whether residential or commercial), followed by the speculative house developer (Graph Three). Local authorities are statistically infrequent claimants. One miserable claimant was a finance house burdened with a variety of unlettable and unsellable commercial properties in a declining industrial area of Central Scotland which it had underwritten as a consequence of an over-enthusiastic – if not ignorant – valuation based upon the wrong premise[ ].

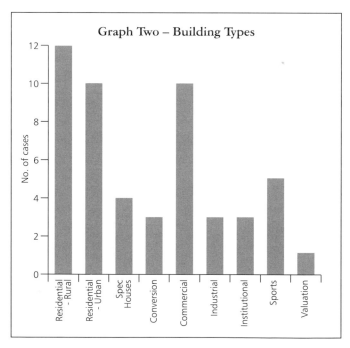

Graph Two – Building Types

Annunciation

The heralding of a problem comes in many ways (Graph Four). In some cases, it was the noise of the thump of a

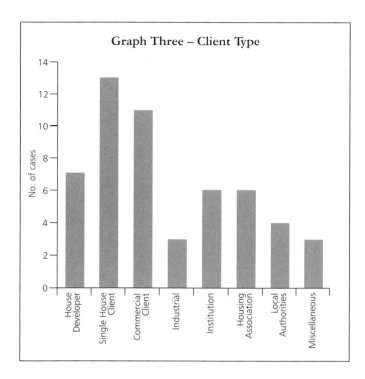

Graph Three – Client Type

In five cases, the trigger for the claim was the pursuit of unpaid fees by the architect, and in three others, a building defect revealed by a storm or gale. Twice the architect learned about the problem through his local newspaper, and in four cases he had the ignominy of the planning authority stopping work on site. In one case, the day before hand-over, the fire officer refused occupancy on the grounds of non-compliance; and in another, the adjoining proprietor took out an interdict during the contract because they were building partially on his land. Any delay during a contract can lead to horrendous costs as did these.

The annunciation of a claim, otherwise, might arise from an unfortunate event – a cliff collapse, a burst boiler, a scalding radiator, slipping swimmer, jamming door, blooming merulius lachrymans, a crack, collapse, or leak. Hotel guests might resent being kept awake by the volume of the karaoke downstairs. Reluctance or refusal by the client to pay a contractor's certificate was almost invariably a premonition of something worse; and there could be no lingering doubt once the client has appointed another architect or – worse – a claims consultant, whatever they claimed by way of benevolent intention.

writ. But it could also come as the telephone call from a friendly rival architect: *'I say, old chap, have you time to visit the xyz that you completed five years ago? I have been asked to carry out minor maintenance, and yesterday when the workmen went up on the roof, it collapsed like a pack of cards. Like to have a decko?'* The response *'shan't, thank you very much'* was the wrong answer. It seems perverse of the architect (and there were two cases like this) to refuse first-hand knowledge of a problem with his building. In both cases the architect damaged his and his insurer's interests by being unable to inspect the problem prior to remedial work by others, and thus made himself vulnerable to what those others would say about his design.

The Claim

What were the claimants seeking? They were seeking to recover costs of remedy, but almost 25% were also seeking a contribution to lost revenue/income or recompense for the contractor's claims where work had been interdicted on site. Speculative house developers who had lost one house here, two flats here, or indeed an entire phase of the development, sought compensation for that loss; as did the office developers with lost rental, and the restaurateur crucial months of operating profits. At least the cinema projectionist was prepared to continue projecting with water dribbling down his neck.

One claim was for the recovery of fees to date, and damages, since the service had become worthless once the project had been aborted for cost overrun. Two of the most appalling cases were the consequence of the issue of an

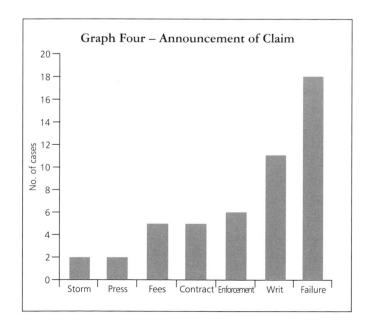

Graph Four – Announcement of Claim

architect's 'Building Society' certificate. The claims were, effectively, for the entire cost of the building construction since their collapsed condition rendered the buildings more or less useless. The risks inherent in issuing such certificates far outweigh the potential fee value. That the outcome was other than wholly catastrophic for the architects can be attributed to the lateral thinking in the settlement agreement[11]. On the other hand, one client realising that it did not show his staff up in such a good light that they had failed to notice that, in scaling up, the architect had converted a housing estate with no windows to the bathrooms – dropped the claim at mutual expense, and re-appointed the architect.

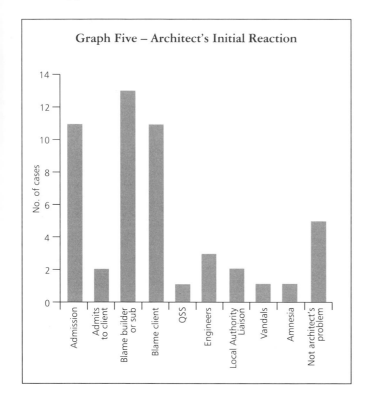

Graph Five – Architect's Initial Reaction

The Architect's Reaction

Graph Five illustrates that there are three equally likely reactions to the receipt of claim: admit fault, blame the contractor or sub-contractor, or blame the client. Two were too honest, and by being so sufficiently indiscreet as to admit it to the client first, they put their policy at risk of voidance. One enterprising architect shifted the blame to local vandals for climbing upon the roof – even though it transpired that the roof had begun to sag and its chipboard dissolve long ere vandals stepped in the

porridge. Three, naïvely assuming that local authority departments liaised with each other, blamed officialdom; five refused to admit any liability, and one was afflicted with selective amnesia.

Matters of Appointment
[RIAS Practice Guide Appointment]

Where forgetfulness is an issue, files should fill in the gaps – save in cases where, as one loss adjuster commented, '*the assured's file is of little value as evidence. Important discussions had clearly not been recorded or confirmed in writing, and even the assured concedes doubts about the history of the project*'. In six cases, the appointment was either not confirmed at all, or was limited – for example to a drawings-only service – in a way that was later disputed, and the architect's position could not be sustained.

The failure to confirm the terms of appointment in writing has been a persistent thread in the RIAS Investigation Committee's annual reports for the last 15 years. These cases demonstrate the consequences. It is not always easy to ring-fence the extent of the professional service. In one claim, the appointment was precise in what was *included*, implying that everything else was excluded. Once problems arose, however, the client sought the architect's insurance cover for defects in the work that had *not* been *included*, but *not specifically excluded*. The lack of precise exclusion, combined with the architect's undoubted interest in the work in question, made his position impossible to defend and necessitated a settlement. If the appointment for a hotel extension were for drawings only, should those drawings have contained details of sound attenuation? Where does a drawing stop and specification begin? Where the architect acts in a role other than that of an architect – such as a cost adviser or valuation surveyor – one reason why their projects became claims was that the terms of what was expected from them were so imprecise that they were judged against the standard of that other discipline. [RIAS Practice Guide Appointment]

In the two sad cases of the architect's certificates, the architects had, by issuing such certificates to purchasers, taken upon their own shoulders a soundness of structure for which they had not been appointed. In one of them, the architect had moved to a different firm after having completed the drawings, and was not around to inspect the construction. He returned to the firm after the project was complete, and had then incautiously signed a certificate without being aware that the new cross-wall, which he had originally specified to be carried down to proper bearing at cellar level, was resting instead on a cellar-full of rubbish and fill. [RIAS Practice Guide Appointment]

The Voiding of the Policy

Such issues bring us, most contentiously, to the issue of voiding the policy. There is little doubt that had the special circumstances of RIAS Insurance Services Ltd not existed, a quarter of these claims would most likely have been rejected – and the majority were at a financial level to bankrupt the architect's office. The matter is *whether the architect has acted in a such way that would damage the interests of the underwriters.* Three failed to notify the circumstance, and one failed to mention the claim upon renewal or transfer to the company. Naturally, they all claimed to have good reasons – the most frequent being *'I thought it was not significant'*, or *'it was a builder's problem'*. They were wholly wrong. The RIAS clause exonerating innocent non-disclosure was the means by which the underwriters agreed to take on these claims, but it was often a very hard-fought battle, and in one case, was only achieved by the architect/chairman of RIAS Insurance Services Ltd threatening to resign[14].

In three cases, the architects injudiciously admitted liability, or agreed to submit to arbitration, without the insurers' consent – and in one case, did so in public. In another claim, the architect heedlessly instructed work knowing that it encroached upon neighbouring territory. He had discussed the matter with the neighbour's agent early on, and thought he had come to an agreement that his client could buy the amount of encroachment from the neighbour's property: but the neighbour's agent changed, the agreement was not in writing, and the new agent wished to make beneficial use of the land upon which the

building encroached. As a consequence, he interdicted the scheme during site works. The underwriters were terminally unimpressed by an architect knowingly building on someone else's land: the action was classified as reckless and put the architect's cover at risk[15].

The certificate issued by the architect to a neighbour for a house that proved broken-backed house and sliding downhill on an underground burn, was so worded that it sounded like a guarantee: *'I certify that the plans and specification of the building and its construction conform to good building practice with the use of sound materials to the satisfaction of the district council'*[16]. Issuing of guarantees is expressly against policy conditions.

'The architect must never forget that he is the intermediate agent between the employer whose interest he is to study, and the mechanic whose rights he is to defend.'

In one project, the architect changed his role from architect to builder during construction and the contract was a total shambles. There was dispute as to whether the client had ever been informed of this change, as nothing was confirmed in writing, and the client was certainly unaware of the implications of the architect certifying himself. Yet, ironically, it was because the architect had failed to notify the client in writing that he was no longer acting as an architect that the company actually covered the case and paid the poor client. For the architect was not insured in his capacity as a builder; but was insured in his capacity as an architect. There was, therefore, a legitimate claim for poor inspection, given the issue of a final certificate and the condition of the building. The ethical issues of such cases – not unusual as circumstances before the RIAS Investigation Committee – deserve consideration[17].

Similarly, an architect acting beyond his competence may find his policy at risk. The architect who undertook a valuation survey of five commercial properties for a building society appears, from the evidence of the file, to have carried it out on the basis of a fairly rudimentary visual inspection: *'Whilst we were not able to examine trading records'*, he wrote *'from observation it was obvious that a good trading pattern exists, and income should reflect this'*. By comparison between what the architect wrote, and what the later expert valuation surveyor concluded, the extent of the gap between the two disciplines became clear. What the architect described as *'a very active trading area'*, the surveyor described more accurately as *'a local economy struggling to recover from major mine closures'*. What the architect had regarded as *'a bituminous felt roof ... in good condition'*, the surveyor described as *'an inferior form of roof construction with short life expectancy'*. What the architect considered to be *'a very viable shopping unit'*, the surveyor criticised as having *'an irregular shape and layout'*. The architect had grossly overvalued the properties, and the insurance company had to pay the building society accordingly[18].

Perhaps the most bizarre case of potential voidance of policy was the one where the architect had undertaken the work for a few neighbouring proprietors in Glasgow. Such was his inadequacy at formalising the nature and scope of both client and brief (never mind a cost-overrun reaching up to 350%), that when the heterogeneous client group in the building next door refused to pay the builder the vastly increased sum, the sheriff held that *the architect himself had become the client*, and was therefore liable to pay the builder. The sheriff's reasoning went like this: *'it was far from clear that the principals (in the contract) had been adequately identified'*. Since there was no adequate identification of the principals, the architect *'had contracted as agent for an undisclosed principal, and was, therefore, personally liable for the contract'*[19]. A suit for debt by a contractor is not, however, covered by professional indemnity insurance as it is not a breach of professional duty: and the initial reaction of the underwriters was to refuse cover.

The voiding of a policy is probably worse for the client than architect. Only exceptionally will the architect's personal assets be sufficient to pay the sums involved – and some clients clearly feel very uneasy at driving professionals to personal sequestration. The fact that RIAS Insurance Services Ltd persuaded the underwriters to provide cover for each of the above exemplify what one opposing solicitor ruefully described as *'very elegant solutions'* – a term normally, and most appropriately, applied to a chess match.

SECTION TWO: THE CLAIMS' CAUSES

*F*ew surprises emerge from the causes of claims, but they can be grouped in a revealing manner. First, there are those deriving from a lack of co-ordination or liaison between disciplines. Second, there are those consequent upon the architect's loss of control – control over something as seemingly simple as site boundaries or as thorny as control over cost. Lastly, claims arise from failings during the process of design and from errors in contract administration, but more important examples come from a lack of careful inspection *at the critical time.*

Cost

'How many fathers of families … have to complain of being led into great and unexpected expenses and justly impute their ruin to an ill-placed confidence and a want of constructive knowledge; or to speak in plainer language, to the ignorance or criminal inattention of their architects?'

Given the mythology about architects being unable to prevent costs overruns, it is reassuring that only 15% of the claims alleged budgetary problems. Yet they were by no means insignificant. The highest percentage increase over the original budget was 350%, and there was a pack of others in hot pursuit. The largest sum sued for – slightly over £500,000 – was an exception since the vast majority of claims were for under £50,000, and only rarely settled for more.

'We are continually reminded of the dreadful consequences of mischievous tendency of defective,

hasty and incorrect estimates; for it is from the consideration of these circumstances that those who wish to build apply rather to builders, who have houses ready constructed to dispose of, than to architects regularly educated for the profession. How many of those who have built under the direction of architects (even in our days) have unhappily had to deprecate the miseries they have been led into by erroneous calculations and mistaken ideas of expense. This is certainly a sore evil.'

Cost overruns could sometimes be attributable to the client. If a client cuts the budget below reason, a warning is insufficient if the architect carries on with a lesser design or material, and it fails. Wishful thinking does neither architect nor client any good. As Dr William Kelly used to say: *'Never do the not-worth-doing'.* Where, for reasons of cost, the client dispenses with other consultants such as mechanical and electrical engineers, beware of assuming that the architect is necessarily an adequately competent substitute. Depend upon it, and trouble may ensue. It is particularly troublesome, however, where both architects and client assume that the former can act as a quantity

Wishful thinking does neither architect nor client any good

surveyor. The architect who is '99% *sure that the costs are on target*' appears with unfailingly regularity in insurance claims. In two claims, where the cost overruns were 33-50% over budget, clients were nudged to the brink of bankruptcy; and in another, the client had to sell a significant additional property to pay for the works.

> *'Young students {should} pay a due regard and consideration to the moral character of the architect in the discharge of his numerous and very important duties, particularly as respects correctness in the estimated expense of the works.'*

As much in a small building or extension, as in a complicated project, a crude square metre (m) rate is a hopeless project management tool. The consequences of reduction in specification to cut costs was a prime factor in seven claims, and the contortions into which the architect was forced to pretend to the client that the substitution would be as adequate as the original were sometimes masterly. There is a danger in client and architect deluding themselves. In a number of recent cases, architect and client agreed unrealistic cost savings. The outturn was as expensive as had originally been forecast, but the contortions that had been required to achieve those phantom cost savings had ended up making the building, in total, more expensive than it would have been. In particular, it is unwise to base economies on the belief that humans could be trained to endure discomfort (see later).

> *'The young Artist {should be} extremely careful as to the expense of his works, and keep in his remembrance the Ephesian Law, by which when an architect received a charge of a public building, he was obliged to deliver an estimate of the expense, and assign over his goods to the magistrates until the work should be completed. If the expense agreed with the estimates, he was rewarded with high and distinguished honours. If it did not exceed more than a fourth part, the excess was added to the estimate and supplied to the public. But if more than a fourth part was expended, his goods were most justly seized to make up the sum.'*

Site or Survey Issues
[RIAS Practice Guide Appointment]

Over 20% of the cases were at least partly attributable to site or survey deficiency. You might have thought that of all things afflicting architecture, the ground on which the project is to stand would be the easiest matter to resolve; or, if an existing building, it would simply be a matter of a good survey. It is perhaps just a trifle careless only to discover that the proposed design fits neither the existing building nor its structure *only once construction has begun*, and that the loss of the original design concept was what the client held most dear. It really is most inattentive to build on someone else's land; and it does little to enhance the architect's standing to insist – as did three – that the culprit was actually the engineer, since it was on the latter's drawings that the encroachment was first made manifest (but which the architect had not spotted when those drawings had been wafted in front of him).

> *'Architecture ... protects us from the shimmering lightnings and the furious tempests, from the heats of the summer and the severities of winter; and by its powers, the comforts, conveniences and refinements of life are increased. Architecture likewise protects us from ambitious neighbours.'*

By their very nature, some developments cause local animosity, particularly speculative housing development.

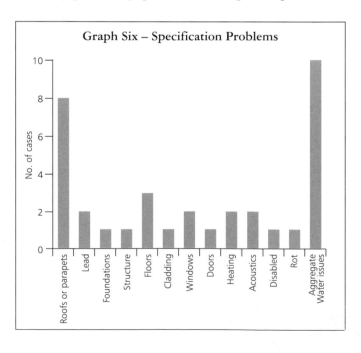

Graph Six – Specification Problems

Depend upon it, stray a millimetre from the site boundary, and an irate neighbour will rumble it. One claim hinged upon the fat point-size of the felt tip pen used to draw the site plan. The fault only emerged when the irate neighbour informed the local newspaper that half a house had strayed[20].

Specification

'To prevent defects in the roof is particularly necessary because troubles generally begin in those parts of the building where they cannot be noticed until the mischief has extended far beyond its original source.'

As was seen from <u>Graph One</u>, almost 50% of the cases involved an error in specification or detail (taken to be Work Stages E, F with a hint of G). <u>Graph Six</u> shows the detail. The majority of specification problems related to the roof; three to floors, two to windows, two to heating systems, with a miscellany of other matters – foundations, rot, structure, doors etc.

'To secure by proper roofing a building effectually and permanently against the repeated attacks of weather and inclement seasons is an important part of the duty of the architect.'

Almost half involved water – ingress through roof, dormer window, parapet, wallhead, window; or inadequacies in disposing of water from showers etc. Two were the consequence of faulty lead specification and two others of changes to the specification during contract – one which reduced the quality, and the other which increased it. Both shared the same feature of inadequate formal recording of the decision at the time. Comparable problems occur if a product has to be changed on site, and no amended specification is issued. In one silly case, the job architect had scaled up the plans inaccurately; whilst in another, the new architect had not been informed, or had not informed himself, that a particular section of a larger project had to be designed to amenity standard.

A recurring *passacaglia* is the old-fashioned Scots habit of leaving specification to the quantity surveyor. Nothing made the late RIAS Past President Arthur Wright more grumpy. Specification is the duty of the architect [RIAS Practice Guide Contracts]. Surely an architect responsible for designing the façade of an important bank in an important town would regard the design, specification and completion of that façade as a matter of particular note? Not always[21]. Not infrequently, critical parts of the specification were left to the builder, and those parts failed. The architect's liability arose from the duty to satisfy him/herself that what was finally provided was fit for the purpose: an obligation made all the more inescapable if the architect certifies the work (of which, see more later).

The autocratic client thought he had sufficient influence to prevent any comeback

Approvals and Grants
{RIAS Practice Guide Briefing & Approvals}

About a quarter of the claims arose from problems with officialdom, through wrong assumptions, carelessness, poor procedures and, sometimes, sheer gormlessness. Four arose when architects working-up contract documentation failed to check that what they were developing conformed to the original planning permission. Having a planning officer interdict a project on site is one of the most expensive causes of claim since a remedy can include taking down, re-specification, and in one case a new structure – all whilst the contractor's clock is running and the clients may be forfeiting occupancy revenue[22]. It defies comprehension how alterations to a grade A-listed building in an outstanding conservation area could have been handed to a technician with no contextual information: such that he specified double-tilt UPVC windows to replace original sash and case, and did not see it necessary to seek planning permission for the change. Perhaps the very autocratic client persuaded the architect that nobody would dare notice or, conversely, that he had sufficient influence to prevent any come-back.

There is a recurrent tendency to believe that where building control has approved plans, they will necessarily have consulted the planning department (or vice-versa) whereas the reality is that the local authority department – or even groups within the same local authority department – might as well exist on separate planets for the amount of co-ordination or collaboration that they achieve. With more justice, an architect believed that if a plan was acceptable to building control it would necessarily be acceptable to the fire officer. Wrong again. Nor did a casual approval by a water board necessarily mean that what was proposed complied with the regulations: and it certainly did not mean that the board accepted any liability for the failure which resulted. Even the issue of a building warrant will not necessarily absolve the architect if the design is incorrect. It is the architect's duty to ensure that the design complies with the law.

It will come as little surprise that the complications inherent in attempting to obtain government grants can prove so sufficiently trying that the financial benefit is overwhelmed by the consequence. In order to qualify for a repair grant, one poor flat occupier had to extend the work by over 300% and did so in the light of the incautious and unfulfilled promise by the architect that the rise in value on completion would more than cover the difference – which is why we know about it. The client probably ended up worse off than when she had started, having had, in the meantime, to endure several years of angst and anxiety. A local authority desiring a new sports building was tempted to expand its ambition by the sports council to a level that it could no longer sustain: and the increase in costs was blamed upon the architect who was then sued for all the abortive costs.

Seeking approvals too late is depressingly common. An architect prepared concept sketches for the viability of a conversion to flats without first discussing the building with the fire officer. Quite rightly, the developer took those sketches to represent the conversion's viability, costed it accordingly and then purchased the building. The fire officer subsequently proved unbending over the matter of a timber stair as a means of escape and the developer consequently lost 20% of his development value[23]. Similarly, highways approval was sought months *after* construction of a housing development began: at which point the developer was compelled not only to spend substantial additional sums for the phases under construction, but to abandon an entire further phase of the development. Failure to appreciate a client's economics and payback period led another architect to manage a restaurant conversion at a pace wholly incompatible with the client's business plan, greatly exacerbated by a late application for planning permission for a historic building in an outstanding conservation area.

One file opens with an exasperated client letter: '*This is the third time that we find ourselves on site on one of your contracts without the necessary authorisation*'. Full building warrant had not yet been received well more than a month after work had started. Only then did it transpire that the architect's interpretation of the necessity for ventilated lobbies in a tenement development was disputed by building control. The latter having the larger battalions, substantial changes were required on site, the consequences whereof were particularly painful[24]. Such matters require resolution in good time. Where the client's timescale sometimes compels an unrealistic stop/go pattern upon a project, the architect must make his or her position clear in writing.

Failure to check is recurring feature. The presence of pipework or electricity close to a site does not necessarily mean that services are immediately available. Worse, however, is where the architect may be tempted to be too helpful to the client by permitting design changes which do not conform with the original planning permission, in the hope that they might not be noticed. Similar instances were not unknown to the RIAS Investigation Committee. If the error can be shown to be inadvertent, the insurance company will provide cover. Should such an act be shown to have been deliberate, the architects are likely to have breached their requirement to show due diligence, and the cover would be put at risk.

Codes & Published Guidance
[RIAS Practice Guide Contract Documents]

'The architect must acquire a thorough knowledge of the qualities of the different species of materials he has to use.'

Since, in over half the claims, the material specified or the detail was inadequate for the intended purpose, the question arises as to whether relevant published guidance was followed. Deviation from guidance, codes or British Standards was alleged in about half, although in one case, the problem was caused by differing interpretation of the regulations between architect and building control. Some problems derived from simple misreading of the relevant document: one from a correct specification but subsequent failure to spot incorrect installation, whilst another from a failure to control adequately a BRE-specified remedy to a problem that had already been encountered. Sometimes, the codes or standards were superannuated. In two claims, the architect had failed to address the particular weather conditions of the site, and specified something more suitable for sunny Surrey. Nothing new in that. The London architects Coe & Goodwin specified Caen stone for the dressings of Dundee Royal Infirmary in 1852; and on that exposed Caledonian estuarial site, the dressings all failed and had to be replaced at great cost. But the law expects indigenous tribes to understand their own environment.

It is important to recognise the significance of published documentation. Virtually none of the organisations publishing standards or codes of practice will accept liability if the specification fails. Whatever reference is made, the responsibility for the performance of the material or detail largely remains with the architect. Where he or she chooses not to follow published guidance, that is not of itself proof of error – demonstrated by the Wester Hailes case, 1983[25]. Following Hunter vs. Hanley,

1957, if the architect can persuade another architect of standing to support his or her judgement in court, and give adequate reasons for deviating from published guidance, his/her decision is likely not to be held negligent per se. But what he/she has to do is to demonstrate an awareness of the relevant information, and have strong professional reasons for dissenting. An architect rejected CP121 in one claim, and opted for a solid, thicker parapet. The expert witness observed wryly: *'The architect has not understood that most of the water penetrates the joints and not the bricks, and merely increasing the thickness of the wall would only have marginal benefit'*. Worse, the damp proof course did not extend the full width of the wall. Saturation was the result[26]. To be ignorant of current practice, or to specify it wrongly, is to risk law suits.

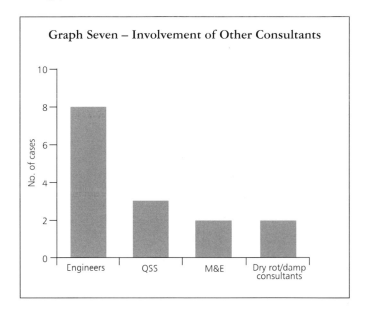

Other Disciplines

Architects do not always stand alone in the face of client wrath. Another consultant (or the lack of one) was germane to the problem or its solution in a quarter of the claims – most frequently the structural engineer, with a supporting cast of three quantity surveyors, two M&E consultants, and one dry rot specialist (Graph Seven). Too much reliance on the engineer (i.e. the latter's drawings inadequately checked), or too little (he was not consulted) had the same result; claim. One architect believed that the dead weight of a factory hatch cover – which was so heavy that it had to be lifted into place by a heavy duty crane –

could withstand anything. The next storm picked it up and tossed it like a frisbee. When eventually consulted, the engineer was massively unsurprised: he had never been asked. Twice, the client thought to save money by dispensing with mechanical and services engineers, and ended up with claims. Architects acting as quantity surveyors, or getting quantity surveyors to act as architects (by taking over the specification) have already been mentioned. But even where they are following their own disciplines, there must be mutual understanding as to work patterns. One claims resulted from the architect's assumption that he would be informed promptly of any cost implications from the manifold architect's instructions issued during the final stages on site, and took silence as good news. However, a few months later, practical completion having been reached, the quantity surveyor finally turned to all those architect's letters on his desk.

Contractual Issues

[RIAS Practice Guide Duties on Site]

> *'Construction is another very necessary and useful part of our art. By the knowledge of construction, the architect is able to direct and instruct the artificers, instead of being controlled by them.'*

Three-quarters of the claims had a primary or secondary cause for claim arising during the contract and/or from the contractual process. They divide almost equally between

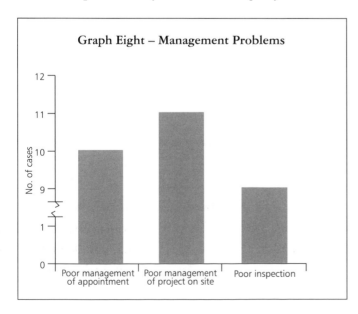

three types of failure (Graph Eight): failure to administer the contract adequately, failure to manage the commission adequately, or failure to inspect adequately. Graph Nine illustrate the principal causes of contractual problem. For example, it often took a claim for the architect to realise that the contractor had deviated substantially from the drawings or specification, and had carried out his own substitution. Very rarely had the contractor done this for altruistic, client-focused motives. Normally it was because their supplier had the substitute in stock, or could obtain it easily, and that the contractor had ordered too late: and it was almost certainly cheaper. None of the seven claims arising from this had been spotted during inspection. In

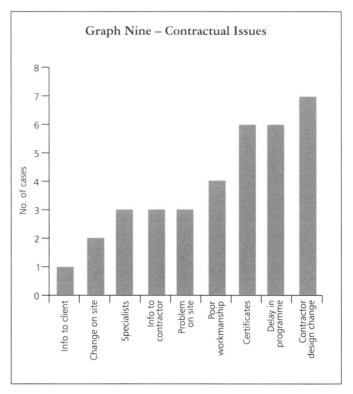

two, the inspector – the job architect – was not the specifier. Four times, poor workmanship eluded the architect – which he had later certified. In all, six times liability attached to the architect by virtue of him/her having certified such work.

It was sometimes just puzzling. An architect, already losing trust in the joinery sub-contractor, was surely perverse not to increase his site inspection visits during that short period when the joinery men were undertaking significant structural alterations. To adhere to a rigid, pre-programmed weekly visit was perhaps taking a risk too far. [RIAS Practice Guide Duties on Site]

One claim involved the contract document where the architect, without taking legal advice, had made an alteration to the contract that could (had the client's lawyer been better advised) have caused appalling financial consequences[27]. One rebarbative claim hinged, ultimately, on the tendering process. The architect received only two tenders for a common repairs project resulting from a repairs notice from the local authority. His suspicions failing to be aroused by the 350% difference between the two, he selected the lesser, and obtained grant for it. As costs escalated during the contract (by approximately 350%) it transpired that only the more expensive contractor had actually seen the repairs notice. Poor communication of this type – or insufficient information to the contractor, failure to inform the client of development on site, failure to confirm the decisions in writing etc. – was not infrequent.

Urgency was singularly absent in four other claims. In one, the primary allegation was cost overrun consequent upon late production of drawings – too late for the QS to cost before the contractor built them; in any case most of the drawings had gone straight to the contractor first. That was hotly denied, on the grounds that the quantity surveyor received all written documentation timeously and that, had he only been alive, he might have been alert to what was going on or at least demanded the drawings to cost them. Sometimes, delays were caused by the difficulties of finding a relevant specialist (e.g. stone mason) to cope with changes required on site.

The Relevant Event

Almost a third of the claims hinged upon which stages of construction required the architect or inspecting officer's presence on site – what legal jargon titles 'the relevant event'. Save in those rare cases where the architect is paid for a supervisory service, the duty is to visit the site from time to time to *inspect* generally the progress of the works [RIAS Practice Guide Duties on Site]. When visits should be made is, theoretically, left up to the architect's judgement, but then the law has the

habit of determining, retrospectively, what might have been deemed to be a relevant event on site worthy of inspection. Some legal cases have defined relevant events – and they have been as various as a site layout on the one hand, to the laying of a parquet floor on the other – based on a subsequent failure. These RIASIS claims indicate that the determination of what is or is not a relevant event depends largely on the architect's judgement. Since the sub-contractor's performance in one claim indicated that critical work by him would merit closer attention than usual, the architect might have been well advised to visit during that process. However, no penalty attached to him, this time, for not doing so; the penalty had attached to the fact that upon taking down, some timberwork, which the architect had designed without re-checking with the engineer, was revealed to be inadequate[28].

If the architects fail to visit during setting out, laying foundations, or when they could inspect cavities for rubbish and wall ties, or check upon primary structural fixing or the specialist sub-contractor work, they may be rendered vulnerable. Installation of fires, of insulation in the roof space and of pipes, of the vapour barrier, of central heating systems, of the DPC, of roof fixing, and of specialist floor laying – would, depending upon the nature of the project, all have benefited from specific targeted inspection. That implies that architects should consider which stages of each project, which installations and the work of which specialists must be inspected, *a priori*, and arrange their contract administration accordingly.

Certification
[RIAS Practice Guide Duties on Site]

Certificates represent trouble. By their issue, the architect is probably taking on to his or her shoulders the responsibility for the visible or patent quality of the work (i.e. what might reasonably have been noticed by a professional person upon periodic visual inspection). The interim certificate seems only to become a qualitative issue if, for some reason, the contract is not completed or the builder goes bankrupt.

Loss adjusters, however, believe the architect to be vulnerable for certifying defective work with either the practical completion or final certificates (for both feature in these files). The architect who failed to notice that the specialist sub-contractor had installed contrary to the British Standard shouldered part of the blame[29]. A naïve architect, outsmarted by a client and builder who colluded and altered details on site which later proved to be defective, nevertheless issued an AI to cover the change and subsequently certified it. Blithely issuing a certificate which takes the contract sum many percentages above that agreed by the client, without that client's prior agreement, may prove problematic.

Practical completion certificates cause other problems. Where the fault is palpable – such as evidential damp penetration – the issue of a practical completion certificate can only act against the interests of the architect. Worse, an architect had recommended the use of a JCT80 contract *where the client had an immovable occupancy date*. JCT80 is incompatible with an immovable occupancy or opening date. Significant palpable building problems were evident on the opening day. However since the client had taken occupation, the contractor insisted on the issue of a practical completion certificate – and the architect's attempt to qualify it did not entirely exonerate him.

The Expert Witness

About half the claims reached the initial stages of arbitration or court proceedings, and the majority required the insurance company to appoint an expert witness – albeit frequently wincing at the cost. Expert witnesses come in all shapes and sizes, and much can be asked of them. One visited the hotel to test the sound attenuation for himself. He slept intermittently. Expert witnesses are to be found on roofs and in basements. Not infrequently, you can infer that the expert witness dislikes the project architecturally, or its method of construction, or certain of its details – but does not let that cloud (always his) judgement. If it is not germane to the claim, he notes it and passes on. It is the expert witness who generally navigates speedily around codes of practice and British

Standards, and is good at details. In two cases, he had to judge from documents alone since the appointment took place only after remedial work had been completed by the client. Generally, the expert witness represents the voice of solidly cautious common-sense. Since the insurance company generally determines upon settlement based upon its own expert witness one is rarely set against another in these claims. There is normally substantial agreement between the objective views of expert witnesses on both sides as to the technical causes of failure. In the one case where there was serious disagreement, that was because there were three of them; and whereas they all concurred with the analysis of the various faults of the project, they disagreed as to which of the faults had contributed to the claim, and what blame might be attributable.

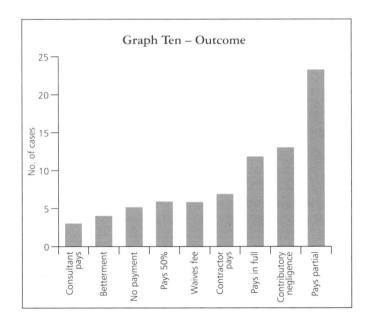

Graph Ten – Outcome

Settlement

The claims files generally compose one-third assessment of the problem, and two-thirds direction towards settlement. Occasionally, the settlement springs unheralded from the page as the company's legal advisor achieves another feat of prestidigitation.

The statistics demonstrate the extent to which the outcome is not foregone. In only under a quarter of the cases did the architect's insurers have to pay the entire sum sued for (Graph Ten). In about half, the architect contributed – sometimes substantially – to the settlement, but seven times in tandem with the builder, three times with the engineer, and once with the quantity surveyor. In six cases, the architects paid nothing – both sides retiring hurt, bearing their own costs. Nor is the level of settlement pre-ordained. The vast majority of claims were settled at 50% or less of the sum sued for at 'the peak'. Speed and ease of settlement depended primarily upon the clients and their (oft-times less than hungry) solicitors. Slightly under half were straightforward; in a number, the clients were very supportive and simply sought remedy for errors – in five cases very quickly indeed. However, an almost equal number of claims were complicated and difficult, and the majority of these latter proved, sadly, to be acrimonious (<u>Graph Eleven</u>).

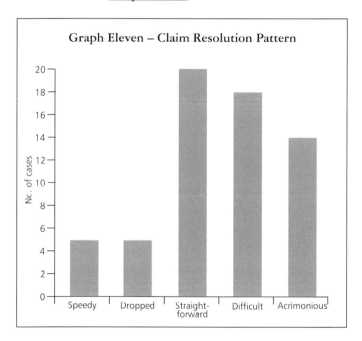

Graph Eleven – Claim Resolution Pattern

Client Issues

In over a quarter of the claims, the clients' own actions contributed to the problem, to the extent that they were held to contribute to the settlement or forfeit part of their claim. That, at least, is what is implied by the terms of the passage to settlement.

In a specific group of claims, it was not so much a matter of culpability for wrongdoing so much as a matter of *betterment*. The final building, after remedy, was in some way better or better built than the original, and it was natural that the client should contribute to that element. The exploration and calculation of betterment (and the negotiation thereof) form one of the many elegancies of these files. It was a more difficult matter where, whilst the betterment was admitted, the client maintained that they had never chosen to have the betterment since they could not afford it. Since this matter never came to court, it is impossible to determine the value that the courts might have given to such an argument.

Where there were issues of culpability that might be translated into an assumption of client contributory negligence, the client *lacunae* are various. The fault, sometimes, was trying to carry out building projects on the cheap – exemplified by a refusal to appoint necessary specialist consultants, or by opting for a drawings-only service, or offering only a token fee; and the client paid for his own cupidity. Occasionally, genuine budget pressures compelled a reduction in specification beyond that which was sensible. Sometimes the fault lay in the client's operational method. Patterns of stop/go, pause, acceleration, indecision followed by urgent action disrupt the logically sequential design process, and usually end up with the imposition of unacceptable time schedules, in which error becomes the norm rather than the exception.

There is then the problem of the extent to which the architect should be able to depend upon a client's expertise. Should developers, converting old buildings into flats (which they had done many times before) have been expected to detect a doubtful fire escape or not? The fact that the settlement was at loss of fees to architect only (i.e. much less than the lost real estate value) implies some acceptance of the point. Should the property manager of a housing association not have been able to spot a block of amenity housing which was neither designed nor built to amenity standards until occupation? Should a finance manager not have been concerned about his employer's refusal to appoint a quantity surveyor over the three critical years that a major scheme was developed?

A client who circumvents the architect to instruct the builder directly is, *ipso facto*, shouldering much of the consequent liability; as indeed is the client who assists the architect in setting out: (an extraordinary scene where each – client and architect, pole, rod and tapes in hand – was relying upon the other for the necessary knowledge and accuracy). Obviously, a client who, knowingly, appoints a professional to a task outside that professional's normal expertise will carry some of the resulting burden (15% in claim 24). Even the client who waxes ambitious and enthusiastic during construction, and becomes vaultingly expansive, will carry some of the blame if at no time did he check, or think to check, that the costs were still what he could afford. The settlement in claim 45 must, therefore, have included a provision for common-sense: that is to say, that no sensible client would have anticipated such a vast extension to his ambition could have been achieved at no additional cost.

It is difficult to generalise about these elegant solutions since, in insurance claims as in fashion, the greater elegance is achieved where it is purpose-designed for the individual. Those with a taste for the arcane might refer to claims 14, 15 and 29.

The underlying causes of claims can probably be grouped under three headings: learning curves, assumptions and procedures. It may be too glib to say that a good architect should never assume: but some of the assumptions in these files were breathtaking in their ambition (Graph Twelve).

Learning Curves

'It may fairly be expected that ere long the respective and distinctive duties of the architect, the surveyor, the measurer, the builder and contractor will be properly distinguished from each other.'

A dangerous assumption is the idea of the architect as universal man, capable of everything – that is, of becoming a valuation surveyor, structural engineer, quantity surveyor, mechanical and electrical engineer, acoustician, lawyer and contractor – without any specific training. Those assuming capability in other disciplines will be judged against the average competence of those other disciplines – and not against the standards of an amateur working knowledge of how they might operate.

[RIAS Practice Guide Appointment]

Acquiring new knowledge (or the failure to do so) can be a problem even within the architectural domain. A new client or a new building type probably requires additional procedural care to avoid any accidents that might derive from the architect's learning curve. With depressing regularity, clients used to tell the RIAS that they were disinclined to be the victim of an architect's learning

curve. The evidence of these claims is that it happens quite rarely, and usually in specification or client liaison. A few claims arose from changes in project personnel where there was a failure to transmit inherited knowledge from one project architect to the next.

Unjustified Assumptions

About half of the claims could be attributed to unjustified assumptions which the loss adjuster found culpable to some degree:

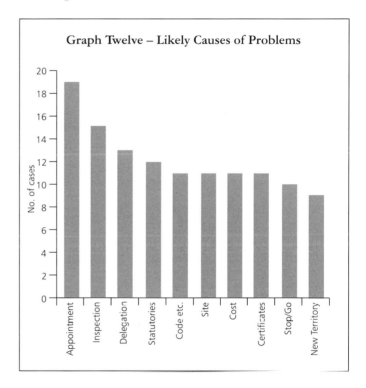

Graph Twelve – Likely Causes of Problems

No. of cases

Appointment, Inspection, Delegation, Statutories, Code etc., Site, Cost, Certificates, Stop/Go, New Territory

Assumptions about the client:

(i) That the client would know the boundaries of the site (claim 5).

(ii) That the client was not in a particular hurry (claim 12).

(iii) That the client would be unfazed by future high maintenance (claim 21).

(iv) That the client would never require access across the roof (claim 26).

(v) That absence of client reaction could be taken as approval (claim 28).

(vi) That friends would appreciate his services (claim 29).

(vii) That the flat's value, once restored, would rise to cover rising costs (claim 27).

Engineering assumptions:

(i)   That you did not need calculations to show that a heavy concrete hatch would never shift (claim 4).

(ii) That simplified structural drawings did not need to be seen by an engineer (claim 16).

Approvals assumptions:

(i)   That building control had talked to planning (claim 6).

(ii) That building control would necessarily talk to the fire officer (claim 9).

(iii) That lack of objection from building control implied satisfaction (claim 19).

(iv) That informal clearance by the water authority represented satisfaction (claim 36).

(v)   That the plan would be acceptable as it had been before, and relaxations would necessarily be available (claim 38).

(vi) That specification by reference to British Standards would be an adequate cover (claim 46).

(vii) That roads permission would be automatic (claim 47).

Site and construction assumptions:

(i)   That the adjacent proprietor would not change his mind (claim 2).

(ii) That services connection would be easily available (claim 11).

(iii) That the extension roof could be a repeat of the main house (claim 18).

(iv) That the building was constructed as designed (claim 20).

(v)   That failures are always the contractor's responsibility (claim 42).

(vi) That the architect's liability would diminish pro rata to the sub-contractor's expertise (claim 43).

Financial assumptions:

(i)   That an underspend remains available to be spent (claim 45).

Constraints in use:

(i)   That behaviour of girls in a shower could be carefully regulated (claim 31).

(ii) That schoolboys in Scotland in January could be expected to shower in rooms with the windows wide open (claim 33).

(iii) That users of a swimming pool would never move changing room benches, or splash their showers (claim 37).

Inadequately briefed for site visits

Procedures

The final group of causes of claims can be combined under the title of faulty procedures, sometimes caused by delegation. The architect frequently attributed the fault to a technician or, in one case, to a *'self-employed associate'*: but in each case, the error by the subordinate had not been not picked up by the partner.

Principal procedural failures appear to be these [RIAS Practice Guide Briefing & Approvals]:

-   failure to communicate adequately with the client;

-   failure to clarify the terms of the appointment;

-   failure to comprehend the client's timescale;

-   failure to comprehend the client's financial circumstances/payback period;

-   inadequate briefing of subordinates;

-   failure to check subordinate's work;

-   failure to check engineer's drawings;

-   misreading of codes and standards;

- contract drawings not checked for conformity with planning;
- failure to scrutinise contractor's drawings;
- inadequate records of decisions and changes;
- failure to communicate cost changes to client;
- failure to communicate design changes to client;
- failure to communicate timescale changes to client;
- inspecting architect inadequately briefed for site visits;
- failure to spot contractor's changes on site.

Both wrong assumptions and faulty procedures could be tackled before disaster by a structured management process within the office: a correct regime of checks, confirmations in writing, adequate communication and the maintenance of a project diary. Drawings for which the architect may have a responsibility should not only be checked carefully but signed off.

Envoi

The most striking feature of most claims files is their banality, their inevitability, and – above all – their avoidability. It is hoped that this monograph might increase the rate of avoidance.

> *'The most simple forms will always be the best fitted and the most proper for the purposes required.'*
> Sir John Soane, Lectures in Architecture to the Royal Academy 1816

Illustration Credits

Illustrations are taken from: *Punch*, 1841; *Punch's Almanack for 1882*, Joseph Smith, 1881; *Mr Punch and the Arts* by J A Hammerton (ed), The Educational Book Company Limited; *The Comic History of England* by G A A'Beckett, The Punch Office, 1864; *Sketches by Boz*, 1836; *Monstrous Carbuncles,* Faber-Castell, 1985; *The Gaberlunzie's Wallet*, 1843; *Mr Punch in the Family Circle* by J A Hammerton (ed), The Educational Book Company Limited; *How to Run a Communal Home* by W Heath Robinson and Cecil Hunt, Hutchison & Co Ltd; *From Pecksniff to the Prince of Wales* by Charles Knevitt, Polymath Ltd, 1990; *The Book of Punch* by Nicolas Bentley (ed), Chatto & Windus, 1955.

Acknowledgements

Thanks are due, first, to Patrick Tyler, Managing Director of RIAS Insurance Services Ltd, without whom this project would not have begun; but also to Eric Hall, founder chairman of the company, John Clark, Arthur Wright and Sandy Brown – early mentors of RIAS practice and the scheme; George Burnet and Peter Anderson; Sebastian Tombs, David Pirie, Frances Stevens, Helen Leng, Mary Ramage, Lena Smith and Susan Skinner.

References

1. *Chickens come home to roost* by Prof George McNab, RIAS Insurance Services Ltd, December 1990.
2. Personal communication from Patrick Tyler, February 1998.
3. The Open Record is an early stage of written pleadings which can be amended as you wish. The Closed Record is the document that can proceed to court, and can only be amended with permission of the judge.
4. *RIAS Members' Handbook*, 1994. Introductory section.
5. *Value or Cost* by Charles McKean, RIAS 1993.
6. *Professional Indemnity Insurance, the First Ten Years* by Charles McKean (ed) Rutland Press (Edinburgh), 1994. See particularly Jeremy Hyne, Director of Professional Indemnity Insurance, ITT London and Edinburgh, *The Underwriter's Perspective*; and David Siddle, Assistant Technical Claims Manager *The claims perspective: is it lower pro-rata in Scotland?*
7. *RIAS Practice Guide,* RIAS, Edinburgh 1988.
8. *Value or Cost* p.12
9. *Professional Indemnity Insurance.*
10. Ibid. p.9
11. Claim 24
12. Claim 21
13. Claims 14 and 20
14. Claim 21
15. Claim 2
16. Claim 14
17. Claim 41
18. Claim 24
19. Claim 29
20. Claim 20
21. Claim 43
22. Claim 17
23. Claim 38
24. Claim 19
25. D Kelly v. Edinburgh District Council and Sir Frank Mears 1983 SLT 145. See also *RIAS Practice Guide, Case Law*.
26. Claim 23
27. Claim 34
28. Claim 16
29. Claim 36
30. Claim 26

Many a slip

Appendix

GUTTERED

A little problem with inspection

The situation

The night it rained heavily on a new factory roof, it leaked badly within. The following day the architects, believing that their design for the roof was satisfactory, noticed that the roofing sub-contractor appeared to have altered their design during construction, and probably caused the leaks. Architects notified prior to any claim, believing they would have no liability. Cost assessed at approximately £3,500 would be attributable to the roofing contractor. The latter hotly denied any liability, claiming that their drawings altering the original design had been checked and thereby approved by the architect. In any case the original architect's design would never have worked, although they had not pointed this out.

Enter the loss adjuster

The loss adjuster's first report concluded that the architect had failed to notice the alterations to the roof design by the roofing sub-contractor, and the alterations to the design remained undetected during construction. The change was indeed the cause of the flood because the straight downpipes were insufficient at the mouth to cope with the heavy falls of water over the large expanse. Loss adjuster concurred with the view that the architect's original design for the valley gutter may never have worked, and assessed the likely cost of remedy at £17,500. He noted that the occupier of the building, a collateral warranty holder, might seek a contribution towards the cost of their professional team.

Final report

As constructed, the drainage system was significantly under capacity for that scale of roof: and because the architect had failed to comment upon the sub-contractor's design, the roofing contractor was entitled to suppose that the architect had approved of the amended design.

The loss adjuster believed the responsibility to be shared: the architect had ample opportunity to check on the design but had not done so: but the negligent act was the sub-contractor's responsibility. He recommended settlement by the architect of 50% of the provisional total costs which had now risen to £30,000, but was reduced by the loss adjusters to approximately £16,000.

Collateral problems

The contract had been a form of design and build whereby the original client had been bought out by another. The industrialist occupier held a collateral warranty from the latter. They, in turn, wished to have their own project management up to inspect and report; and sought to have their costs of c.£12,000 covered as well.

Settlement

The architect was adjudged 50% liable for the contribution towards loss, jointly with the sub-contractor, the loss being calculated as the remedial work plus the collateral warranty holder's expenses (approximately 40% of the total).

Lessons

* An architect accepting design responsibility for a building project is expected to check and verify all design input (particularly where that design alters his original).
* The inspection must be thorough. The alteration to design had not been noticed on site, though, to judge from the correspondence, the inability of the gutter design to cope with the sudden heavy downpour was almost instantaneously perceptible.
* Note the delays and expenses caused by the difficulties of agreeing settlement with the collateral warranty holder.

TRESPASS

Overcoming the site boundary problem by a subtle use of cantilever

The difficulty

Architect informs brokers of a probability of a claim resulting from an interdict issued upon a building contract on the grounds of a small encroachment of adjoining land belonging to the adjacent proprietor who alleges that the encroachment will prejudice further development. The site was not large enough for the building in question, and architects had been authorised to liaise with neighbouring proprietor who had sold a strip of land. Four months *after* the contract began, the architect received a telephone call from the proprietor alleging concrete slab foundations encroachment beyond the area of purchase. One month later, he issued an interdict.

The architect's position

Architect admitted awareness that the foundations encroached from receipt of drawings, but considered it of no significance in the light of his earlier discussions with the adjacent proprietor, (none of which had been confirmed in writing). However, the adjacent proprietor had prepared a new scheme for the adjoining site of which architect was unaware, which would now be prejudiced by encroachment. The architect had been aware that there would be an encroachment at all material times, but claimed that responsibility for encroachment was that of the structural engineer who had prepared the drawings.

The loss adjuster

Loss adjuster ruled the architect liable on the grounds that he had the option of rejecting the engineer's submission. Although the adjoining proprietors had been informed of lodgement of warrant and planning drawings, they claimed they had never received the notification letter, and a study of the drawings would not have revealed the necessity for encroachment. Loss adjuster recommended settlement on best possible terms, suggesting replacement of foundations by cantilever, at approximately £20,000.

Voidance of policy

Underwriters were dismayed to learn that the architect had proceeded with development in full knowledge of inevitable encroachment. They wished to subject the policy to a doubling of the policy excess, since the architect owed a duty of care to the insurers in the exercise and conduct of their professional activities. Was deliberately constructing on someone else's site a breach of good faith so as to void the policy? The broking company pleaded that adjoining proprietor might have expressly or impliedly agreed to the encroachment, but any negligence consisted in not obtaining any written permission: believing it would be a formality.

Underwriters submit the case to legal opinion which concluded:

a)   Action against adjoining proprietor impossible through lack of confirmatory documentation and

b)   However unwise, architect's actions could not be repudiated on the grounds of being reckless or unreasonable. No evidence that the architect took a deliberate decision to proceed with the design which had a potential claim risk.

Settlement

Underwriters accepted liability in full on the grounds that they had agreed to be bound by the legal opinion of a firm which enjoyed a 'profound appreciation of the court's likely attitude'. Settlement was at approximately £31,000, of which 9/10ths were the contractor's costs and delay claims; and only 1/10th money due to adjoining proprietor. No claim against the engineers, although they have to redesign at cost.

Lessons

*   Always record discussions and confirm agreements in writing.
*   Never make assumptions as to adjoining proprietor's intentions (which might change). Only by a near miss was this policy not voided on the grounds of being reckless or unreasonable.
*   Underwriters may void if architects decide to proceed with a design which has a high potential claims risk.
*   Always check engineer's drawings since the authority is that of the architect.

Moral

Underwriters may void a policy if an architect deliberately embarks upon a design with a high potential claims risk.

THAT SOGGY FEELING

Damage to the roof was caused by vandals

The situation

Architects inform insurers that they have been joined as a second defendant in an action for roof failure by a client against the builder. The client claimed that the chipboard roof collapsed because it had been softened by moisture due to inadequate ventilation.

The architect's position

The ingress of water was due to a collapsed roof: the roof being of chipboard whose collapse caused the felt to crack allowing water to penetrate. The architects were surprised at being joined to the action since they had already been called back by the client to assist with remedial works.

Tongue-and-groove chipboard was reasonably fit for the purpose for which it was to be used, and a vapour barrier was indeed installed although not referred to in the specification. The damage was caused by vandals removing lead flashing from the main building and (so it was guessed) using the failed roof as a means of access and escape, and indeed probably dumping the lead down on to it. (Note: this was really swinging the lead. The failed roof faced a public road, whereas there was an easier and more private roof for vandals on the far side.)

Confusion as to what was actually built began to emerge. The architects remembered a vapour barrier and recollected specifying Coolag, but did not recall having seen it. It was not in the specification. Lawyers concluded that the pursuers had raised a speculative case and that liability should be repudiated.

Enter the expert witness

In presence of the expert witness, the defective roof was cut open to reveal chipboard to be soaking, no Coolag, and lacking the ventilation that he would have expected in cold deck construction. Since the contractors were no longer involved, it required a court order to produce their documents.

The expert witness a) concluded that contract information revealed changes of intention and some inconsistencies; b) found no AI confirming the addition of the vapour barrier; c) considered that, whilst it was not unusual for reliance to be placed upon the expertise of competent builders for the resolution of details, *'the roof was too important an element of the building for it not to be fully designed and specified by the architect'*; d) concluded from the specification that inadequate attention had been given to available guidance: e.g. BRE Digest 110; BS5250; BRE Digest 180; BRE Digest 221.

Expert witness disagreed that Coolag incorporated its own vapour barrier; manufacturers confirmed that a separate and additional vapour barrier should be laid immediately below. The cold roof included no provision nor ventilation to the outside air. Expert witness concluded that the preliminaries clause referring to materials, goods and workmanship was unsatisfactory. It was insufficient to call for the best quality of their respective kinds and overall compliance of British Standards. *'For example, the Standards referring to roofing felts, BS747, describes 21 different bituminous felts, each suitable for a particular application. In order to control properly the quality of work on site, the architect must provide precise information to the contractor.'* Since chipboard loses strength when wet, it was an unwise choice for roof decking where there would always be a risk of moisture penetration or condensation.

Summary

a) Failure to provide adequate specification for roof construction in accordance with advice and guidance available at the time;
b) A discrepancy between specification and drawings left unresolved;
c) A failure by the contractor to comply with either the specification or the drawings which remained undetected by the architect.

Settlement

Lawyers concluded this case should be settled on the best terms available.

Lessons

* Always be conversant with contemporary documentation.
* Resolve any conflicts within the contract documentation.
* Check that what is built does not differ materially from what was specified.

BLOWING YOUR TOP

'Incapable of withstanding the wind speeds that could reasonably be contemplated …'

The difficulty

Over a year after the architect had constructed two enormous access hatches in the roof of industrial premises, a severe November gale blew one off which soared across the site and immolated itself against the oil tank. Luckily, the oil tank refused to respond in kind.

The architect's position

The roof hatch was huge. Although the architect called it a biscuit tin lid, it was 6.5m x 3m, required a crane for installation, and was so enormous that the architect had presumed that its own deadweight would be sufficient to keep it in place. He had worked with this particular client over many years on general repair, maintenance and upgrading. His brief was to provide access hatches to allow major maintenance work to be undertaken without dismantling the machinery (as it always had been in the past); so the hatch had to be sufficiently large for machinery to be removed or replaced through it by crane. Since there was no money to strengthen the existing roof, the extent of the hatch and its weight was governed by the roof's structure. The insurance company sensibly allowed the architect to install immediate fixing to the surviving hatch, and the slight risk of admitting liability that this action had incurred paid off almost immediately with the return, the following week, of an even worse gale.

Interim report

When the architect consulted structural engineers on the problem, the latter advised that the hatches had been under-designed since they were incapable of withstanding the wind speeds that could be reasonably contemplated in that area. The architect accepted his judgment, and (in the light of the circumstances) so did the insurance company. The destroyed biscuit tin lid was re-fabricated and hoisted back by crane. Additional security to both was provided in the form of guy ropes which secured the hatches to the walls. That method of fixing still allowed the clients easy removal, access and repair and maintenance.

The finding

The loss adjuster was not entirely convinced by the structural engineers' argument that wind of that speed and force could reasonably be expected at the site, but agreed to concur. He considered contributory responsibility by the client, in terms of the restraint caused by the condition of the roof. However, in the light of the solution of using guy ropes, he concluded that that solution could have been considered *ab initio*. The introduction of guy ropes was at the expense of the client (in that the client would always have had to pay for them) and the insurance company paid for the rebuilding and the re-erecting of the destroyed hatch and related minor damage.

Lesson

The architect assumed that the large object with a heavy dead weight requiring lifting by crane would of itself be sufficiently immovable by the forces of nature. But he does not appear to have checked.

BACKLASH

The architect seduced by the precision of the client's delineation of site boundaries

The situation

An architect, pursuing a fee from a house developer for work on house proposals, is warned of a counterclaim alleging negligence.

The architect's position

The architect was certain that he had no liability. He admitted that the developers had indeed incurred extensive costs, but only as a consequence of their errors made in their execution of the works, which, he thought, they were hoping to recoup through his insurance.

The allegation

The developers claimed that the site plan prepared by the architect was inaccurate in measurement and site level, resulting in both cost and loss of profit, which they took another 15 months to specify adequately, and only then as a defence against the architect pursuing his claim for substantial fees.

The claim

The site had been measured by the architect and one of his clients, joint partner in the development company. The client indicated boundaries on site. The plan submitted for permission by the architect indicated a site 14m longer than it should. Instead of laying out the entire site first, the client began the construction of the first two houses before realising that the tighter site boundaries made the difference between a profitable development and an unprofitable one. The site plan that received planning permission was substantially different from that later prepared by the client for the title deed (necessary for the exchange of land with the adjoining proprietor). Although the architect then informed the client of the difference, neither appreciated the implications of the reduced dimensions. Since the architect was not instructed for any of the building works, he was in no position to advise on the consequences.

The issue

Was the architect entitled to rely on the boundaries he was shown by the client? Was the client prudent in failing to set out the entire site before beginning work on the first 3 houses? Could the client have been held to have known about the reduced site by virtue of the architect's letter and their participation in site measurement? Was there contributory negligence? The counterclaim, £35,000, neither verified in detail nor tested in court, was approximately 5 times the architect's fee claim. The insurance company concluded that, in the absence of written documentation, the matter would be decided by which witness the sheriff chose to believe. Eventually, the insurance company pressed the defenders (the clients) to a closed record with intention to trial, although the latter, still seeking to change their pleadings, were evidently not keen for the case to go to trial. They wished only to be relieved of the duty to pay the fees. The insurance company was advised by an expert witness that, whereas the fees had been legitimately earned, there was sufficient substance in the defenders' counterclaims to merit concern.

Resolution

Four years and one month after notification, the case was settled. The defenders dropped their counterclaim in return for the architect dropping his claim for fees. However, the insurance company paid the architect 50% of his claim for fees, as compensation for dropping the claim and avoiding a potentially greater liability both through the irrecoverable costs of a lengthy trial and the counterclaim. The architect expressed his appreciation of the work that went into achieving the result.

Lesson

There was an error on the site plan for which the architect had responsibility, unless he had made it clear that he was relying on the client's indication of site boundaries. When discovered later in the preparation of the title deed, the implications were never drawn adequately, or early enough, to the clients' attention. Had he done that, the claim might have failed. The potential consequences in terms of lost profit to the developer would have far outweighed the outstanding architect's fees since he was at least partly liable for the financial consequences of actions based upon his inaccurate plan.

A SWINGING TIME

The difficulty

The architect notified the insurance company about the possibility of a claim relating to a hotel refurbishment with two press cuttings reporting a council's enforcement action against the hotel and its co-proprietor, the local laird, for the installation of single-swing, top-hung, double-glazed windows. The hotel was A-listed in an outstanding conservation area. In a programme of converting smaller bedrooms into larger bedrooms with en-suite facilities, dilapidated and draughty windows were to be replaced, on the condition that the replacement was to be like-for-like. The 3 month programme was completed, on contract, by early spring. The planning office rang to enquire whether permission had been obtained for the installation of the new windows, drawing attention to the fact that sash and case windows had been replaced by top-hung windows. A letter the following day warned that unless the windows were reinstated to their former type, or retrospective consent obtained, enforcement action was probable. Retrospective listed building consent for the entire refurbishment was immediately applied for by the architect. On learning of its refusal, he notified the insurance company.

Sudden appearance of the planning officer ...

The architect's position

Although it was accepted that the 21 windows differed from the existing ones, the architect considered that the frames he specified were not material alterations requiring permission other than building warrant approval, which had been received. He found it odd that one department (Building Control & Environmental Health) should accept the proposals, whilst another department opposed them. Furthermore, he now discovered that the window installed by the contractor was not that specified by his technician (although the differences between the two were not such as to have made much difference. It might make a difference, however, to whether or not the contractor should assist with the cost of replacement).

Further developments

The district council refused retrospective planning permission for both windows and internal refurbishment; their focus was upon the new windows, which significantly detracted from the visual appearance and the integral character of the building and its area. The loss adjusters recommended against appeal, since good relationships might be damaged, and the appeal would probably be turned down. The technician in control of the project was unaware of any requirement for listed building consent. His instruction to the contractor had been for all windows to be replaced with double-swing sash and case style ... and to be double-glazed. Those installed were single-swing; when some time after installation, the technician noted the windows were not of the double-swing type, he concluded that to insist on replacement with those originally specified would have been unwarranted.

Enter the laird

The laird, having delivered himself of some opprobrious comments about planning committee members and their ancestors, considering that the windows did not detract from the visual characteristics of the building, decided unilaterally to appeal (despite the fact as the loss adjustors commented acidly that the costs of pursuing such an appeal would be prohibitive in relation to the anticipated window replacement costs). The loss adjusters were concerned that unnecessary costs might arise if the appeal were unsuccessful, and obtained the laird's confirmation that any additional costs would be borne by him.

The judgment

The Judgment of Solomon was received almost exactly 12 months later. The appeal was dismissed in fairly trenchant terms. The reporter rehearsed carefully the appellant's view that when shut, the new windows were similar to those they had replaced, and that the false astragals were aesthetically in keeping with the building and the original style. He found them unacceptable: substantially different, lacking the stepped profile of the original, the false and UPVC astragals were a poor imitation. The character of the building and of the related conservation area was seriously harmed.

Action

Six months later, negotiations with the contractor were far advanced: the windows were to be replaced, the contractor was to bear a one-third contribution to those costs (for installing the wrong ones in the first place), and there would be a small contribution from the salvage of the removed windows. With this plan in progress, the council had agreed to take no further action with regard to the internal alterations. Two-and-a-half years after notification, therefore, the matter was settled at a final cost of almost 10 times less than that which had been originally forecast.

Lessons

* This is a classic case of an inside-out matter. In focusing upon the day-to-day internal upgrading, the legislative status of the building had been overlooked; and the implications of the work were only noticed when some of it (the windows) impinged upon the façade.
* The person running the project clearly enjoyed a limited role. The architect saw the project as a matter of resolution of technical problems through building control without any planning implication: but does not appear to have checked.

WHEN FRIENDS FALL OUT

The situation

A hurt letter from an architect to a client upset that a hotel owner holds him responsible for alleged acoustic problems between bedrooms and bar in a recently extended hotel.

The architect's position

The acoustic problem in the hotel was nothing to do with him, because he had never been asked to provide a full architectural service for the hotel owner. He had been asked to supply a drawings-only service on a low hourly rate for a local builder/works organiser: a commission which implied no inspection duties. The hotel owner (a professional person himself) would pay for no more than a cut-price truncated service. The builder was largely responsible for materials and specification, and methods of working. Once client and builder fell out during construction, the architect visited the site once as a favour to discover that, during construction, client and builder had agreed to reduce specification including sound-proofing; and that (squorrocks!) the client had installed loudspeakers in the bar.

Enter the client's expert witness

Sound attenuation between the bedrooms and other spaces was evidentially poor and could cost over £14,000 to remedy and even then be only palliative. The architect's charges could not be held to imply a full professional service, but the implications of sound transmission should have been comprehended within the provision of a drawings-only service.

The architect's defence

The architect concurred with the technical findings of the expert witness, in general, save that his service only required conformity with building regulations, which was achieved. His direct briefing from the hotel owner was minimal in terms of the use of rooms for special provisions, and even those instructions were diluted through the builder. He had made no written records of instructions or details of the brief, and remembered only vague discussions about the possibility of noise with the builder, who had since died.

Enter the insurer's expert witness

The insurer's expert witness, who slept in the hotel overnight, drew attention to the confusion as to who was the client and responsible for briefing the architect: and criticised the total lack of documentation. He concluded that the sound attenuation on the building had been solely to domestic standard, with a failure to appreciate the different sound requirements likely in a hotel. The architect did not disagree with this analysis, but yet again pointed out to his restricted service, and the fact that the builder had changed specification during building with the client's agreement. The expert witness concluded that the remedial work if it was to be at all satisfactory could prove to be very expensive if it was not to be palliative.

The loss adjuster's view

In the absence of documentation, the facts could only be proved finally in court. The absence of formal documentation, and the likelihood that the

... remembered only vague discussions about noise from the bar ...

sound specification would be accepted by the court as domestic instead of that appropriate for a hotel, would leave the architect at least partially vulnerable. Faced with possible remedial costs of £20,000 or more, they recommended a negotiated settlement to a maximum of £5,000, which to their surprise proved acceptable.

The architect's grievance

The architect felt let down by the insurance company, by the RIAS in nominating an expert witness, and by the decision to settle. He assumed that it was based upon the insurance company's desire to minimise potential financial damage, rather than fight on a matter of principle. He failed to see that his matters of principle were, in fact, upheld by the small amount of the settlement. In the absence of any formal confirming documents of appointment relating to the nature of the client, or the nature of the building, it could have been held by the court that his drawings service should have made adequate allowance for the sound attenuation implications of the use of the building as a hotel. All other matters for which he had disclaimed responsibility were tacitly accepted in a settlement barely one-fifth of the likely cost of producing full appropriate sound attenuation.

Lessons

* Don't do it.
* Confirm appointments in writing.
* Establish formal brief definition from a defined client.
* Ensure that the client understands the consequences of a restricted service.

Moral

Beware a client who wishes to cut corners by getting professional services on the cheap, design is devalued by treating the architect as a subcontractor to the builder: and in taking away from the architect any duties of specification. In short, the client probably got what he had paid for.

On the other hand, an architect who fails to define the extent of his service, to confirm it in writing, to identify his client, or even the purpose for which he is undertaking design work, is laying himself very bare indeed.

A straightforward task of producing a drawings-only service up to building regulations standard will not exonerate the architect if these drawings prove not to be fit for their purpose.

A WEIGHTY PROBLEM

The situation

An adjoining proprietor's architect, having lead roof problems, asked to see copy of a technical report commissioned two years earlier for the adjacent roof. The architect of the adjacent roof realised that the Lead Development Association had never submitted their report and had concluded that there was no problem. Upon its receipt, the horrified architect lodged a notification of claim.

The architect's position

The architect had been responsible for the creation of study bedrooms within an old building. Certain minor problems, principally as a consequence of change of client specification during contract, had raised a question of condensation and/or leaks. Since the roof consisted of steep slated mansards to each side with an almost flat lead roof between, a report from the Lead Development Association was commissioned.

The report

The report identified design faults in the roof which, even though there may be no present failure, would lead to failure in the future. The guides contained in *Lead Sheet & Building – a guide to good practice* (1978 edition) had been misread by the technician. Lap joints used across the fall would be liable to water penetration. Because of the shallow fall of the central section of the roof, a 50mm height step should have been used. Furthermore, a bituminous felt – the wrong underlay – had been used. In circumstances of heat, it could have the result of bonding the lead to the roof's structure which, inevitably, would lead to cracks in the lead as a consequence of differential thermal movement. The insured's expert witness, a university department of building, studied the specification and identified two principal areas of concern. The lapped joints for a near-flat roof would be susceptible to wind-driven rain and capillary action; and the risks of the bituminous felt underlay were as stated by the Lead Development Association.

The inspection

An inspection was duly held with opening up. The roof had been properly laid according to the specification and drawings, and was in good condition. Yet all lapped joints were wet for their full width. The roof was only watertight due to the wrongly specified bituminous felt underlay forming an impervious layer.

Action

The case was unusual in that it dealt with a likely future problem, rather than the consequences of an existing one. Disclosure was made to the client, and rebuilding of the roof was undertaken. For various reasons, the contract was delayed, and the final costs also included a loss of rental for the rooms below for an entire season.

The technician had misread the Code of Practice

Lessons

* In determining negligence, the architect has to demonstrate that he had had recourse to relevant guidance and advice. That was so in this case.
* There is no absolute requirement to follow guidance and advice. The expert witness stated that, although the specification departed from recognised practice, *'this does not necessarily mean that the roof will not function as designed and intended'*. The architect, having regard for guidance and advice, may nonetheless deliberately use his professional judgment to depart from it. Thereafter, the test is the test of result.
* In this case, the technician had simply misread the guidance. It is curious that such a palpable departure from good practice was not picked up by the contractor or subcontractor during construction.

Moral

The case implies that the practice and/or technician had no great familiarity with lead roofs since otherwise good practice would have been known. Moving into uncharted technical territory justifies more stringent checking procedures.

A BURNING ISSUE

To neglect the fire officer is to play with fire

The situation

Property developer writes to the architect holding him responsible if further works are required to satisfy the fire master before a tenant can occupy recently converted premises. The quantum is indeterminate, but the issue appears to be means of escape and isolation of hall and stair.

The architect's position

The architect was appointed to upgrade and convert an existing Grade A Listed terraced building as shell works. Formerly in ecclesiastical use, the building was to be refurbished as offices, and contained outstanding interiors. The appointment specified the architect's duty to include the provision of any information required for the approval of any statutory authority.

The issue

At a site meeting the status of doors giving on to the stairwell was raised, and the necessity to check confirmed. A meeting was held the following day with building control and the fire brigade from which consultation the architect believed that when a building warrant was granted, no additional works would be required by the fire master. He further believed that the building control department necessarily liaised with the fire department. The architect commented ruefully in hindsight, this was obviously not the case. Building control had required no particular changes because the arrangement of stair and doors was as existing, and no alterations were proposed to change that status. The fire master was never approached separately but, in any case, would be reluctant to become involved prior to the issuing of a building warrant, in order to avoid time wasters. Existing alarm systems, fire alarm and smoke detectors were rewired and upgraded as part of the works.

The fault discovered

Practical completion was achieved in approximately six months, after which it was visited by a representative of the fire master, six days before occupation by tenants. Three months later, the tenants were issued with a written list of requirements, within the terms of the fire Precautions Act 1971, including upgrading of all doors to fire resistance, installation of automatic door closers, infill of ventilation panels above doors, and the treatment of all timber wall linings with fire-resistant material. There were further requirements regarding detection and extinguishing apparatus, and the display of signs. The latter the developer was able to pass on to the tenant. The loss adjuster recommended a reserve £20,000, and the work was instructed.

Resolution

The contractor was prepared to undertake the work at cost, as a favour to the architect: and it was speedily completed. Taking into account the architect's excess, the final cost to the insurance company was barely 25% of the reserve.

Peculiarity

The property developer had originally written to the architect stating that he should not have to be put to additional expense for the fire works. How do you define additional expense? There might have been loss of rental, or the works might have proved to be more expensive than they would have been originally, or there might have been costs for loss or disturbance. None of these factors appear to have been the case in this instance. Consequently, the insurance company paid for the installation of items in this building which the client would have to have paid for anyway. Alternatively, the client might claim that there was only a fixed sum available for the entire contract, and he would have diverted money towards these fire works, had he known about their necessity, and away from other works such as redecoration. It is a moot point.

Lessons

*   The fire master must be negotiated with separately from building control, and a check made after building warrant that all his requirements have been taken into account.
*   Responsibility for dealing with the fire master should be identified, and a checking procedure established.

INFIRM EXTENSION

'The foreman's found some tree roots under the north-west corner'

The situation

Four-and-a-half years after the construction of a single-storey kitchen extension to a home for the elderly, the architects (who had incorporated the firm previously responsible for the work) received formal notification of cracking on the wall nearest the boundary. Civil engineers recommended underpinning.

The architects' position

Having clarified that they continued to carry liability, the architects excavated the files. Since the building was only a single-storey construction, and the site was restricted, no trial pits were deemed necessary. When, during the early part of the contract unusually deep black earth had been identified on part of the site, the contractor had been instructed to widen the foundation at that part. Liability was therefore denied.

The client's engineers' report

Test pits were dug. The extension, constructed of a masonry perimeter wall with a flat roof and concrete flooring, was founded on soil comprising sand, black earth, tree roots etc. It was not surprising that settlement had occurred.

Enter third parties

The insurers included the contractors as first third party. Then, the senior technician who had run the job (inadvertently referring to it in his correspondence as a '*kitch extension*') recalled that the stone boundary wall, at a distance of approximately 1m had been substantially reinforced under a separate later contract specified by independent engineers. Should the engineers not be brought in as a second third party? However, when the writ was issued 18 months after the initial notification, it named only the architect.

The insurer's expert engineer's report

The expert witness noted that the builder had not been instructed on the proper course of action i.e. to continue excavation down to a normal firm bearing stratum. Identification of the poor load-bearing capacity did not require specialist knowledge. In addition, he found that the separate underpinning of the boundary wall had not been undertaken in accordance with recognised codes of practice, and had had an undermining effect on the footings of the kitchen extension.

Efforts to bring in the wall engineers for half the claim proved unsuccessful, although they did make a contribution and paid their own legal costs. The builders were absolved after the foreman confirmed he had pointed out the problem to the architects' technician. The technician had not, however, informed the partner, and had not instructed the contractor adequately.

Outcome

A settlement was negotiated without any admission of liability on the part of the architect. The architect was criticised for inadequate instruction to the builders and it is possible that this argument would have succeeded.

Lessons

* Junior staff must report regularly, and confer with partners on questions of judgment.
* The objectives and programme of site visits should be planned with care.

A RIGHT GUDDLE

'... the loss of aesthetic appeal was impossible to quantify'

The situation

Clients notify a claim for the exceptional costs of electricity connection charges to a converted cottage: not having been warned, they had made no allowance for them.

The clients' position

The connection charge was only the tip of an iceberg of grief. The architects' budget cost, of which they were 99% sure (implying that a quantity surveyor had assisted in its preparation), was over 33% out. The clients might never have bought the property had they known the real likely cost, or that they would have to delete the renovation of an entire wing (as they did). The architects had made no enquiry about electricity supply until site works had begun. Only three months into contract were they informed that the costs of an adequate supply would be c.£5,000, too late for the clients to make appropriate provision. Lastly, against the clients' express authority, the architects had instructed the contractor to raise the roof on the west wing to the same height as the main building, leading to a design which they disliked since it ruined the symmetry of the ensemble.

The architects' position

The architects admitted knowledge of their clients' tight budget. They had seen electrical cables running to the site, and had assumed that reconnection would be a simple matter. They had not taken the precaution of telephoning the local board to enquire. The clients' wish for the wing's roof to be lower had been based upon an inaccurate survey since the roof could no longer be lowered significantly (the difference being marginal). The architect had concluded that all roofs should be the same height.

Possible risk

There was concern that the claimants might have decided to buy the property relying on a guessed valuation which turned out to be in material error. The quantity surveyor's assessment had been taken on a very casual basis in the course of conversation related to restricted items.

Proposed settlement

The clients remained deeply disappointed with the service which they had received, but conceded that financial loss for the roof design and loss of aesthetic appeal was impossible to quantify. Had the clients realised they would have to pay for electricity connection, they would have changed their method of heating (the capital cost of connection would have been lower if more electricity was used in house). The matter was settled for the entire additional costs of electricity connection plus something for inconvenience and costs.

Lessons

* A permanently aggrieved client is good neither for the architect nor for the profession as a whole. This catalogue of disaster has provided one.
* The cavalier estimate upon which the clients purchased the property (accompanied by the phrase 99% sure, and hinting that a quantity surveyor had been consulted) was inadequate for the purpose, incompetent in result, and potentially disastrous to all parties. Making guesstimates is unwise.
* If the client refuses to incur the cost of a QS, make sure that is recorded and the client warned of possible consequences. Trying to be a cost expert when that is not part of your skill is unwise.
* The survey of the derelict property contained a flaw sufficiently serious to cause deep client resentment in the matter of appearance. The clients had been enticed by a design that proved impossible but was not informed about the subsequent alterations. Taking clients for granted is unwise.
* The architects having seen old electricity cables, assumed a connection would be easy. They never bothered to check. Taking the availability of services for granted is unwise.

COUNTERCLAIM VULNERABILITIES

Insufficient account taken of doubts about the acceptability of an extension to a listed café

The situation

An architect, pursuing a client in the guise of four separate companies, for four sets of non contentious fees, is informed of the client's intention to sue in counterclaim through a fifth company for failure of service and loss of profit therefrom.

The architect's position

There had been a problem with the counterclaim project – namely the extension of a listed licensed café into a courtyard with conservatory. However, since the client as an individual had appointed the architect, the counterclaim through a company was therefore invalid.

The client's claim

The claim, for approximately £50,000, represented three months' lost trading resulting from late completion in works to a premises involving a shopfront, dining area and conservatory in a listed building in an outstanding conservation area. Despite being warned by the conservatory supplier about the proposed installation, the architect had not made applications for listed building consent, planning permission and building warrant. Any architect of reasonable skill and care would have had the necessary permissions ready in time.

The architect's case

Verbal instructions from the client changed from time to time. A dining room changed to a conservatory etc., caused confusion between the specialist conservatory supplier, the client and the architect. The licensing board had originally accepted the use of the garden as a dining area, not a conservatory or casual area. Replies to the architect's correspondence had not been received, there were no previous requests for drawings, and allegations of delay were denied. The client had unilaterally terminated the architect's appointment without prior intimation.

Legal analysis

The architect might not be able to deny liability on the grounds that the client had acted as an individual rather than a company, in view of his knowledge that the client was acting as a company agent. The client had indeed changed his mind. But whether the architect was to wait for the client to confirm if the change would prevent the grant of a licence before submitting plans, or was to proceed anyway as alleged, was unclear.

Proposed settlement

The client was persuaded to abandon the action against the architect with a settlement for 50% of the outstanding fees on the other matters. If not, they would litigate all the way. The architect lost a part of his outstanding fees in return for abandonment of the counter claim. Both architect and insurance company concluded that it represented an economic and sensible result for the insurers and the insured.

Conclusion

That the architect had to suffer any forfeiture of fee was the consequence of the uncertainty as to responsibility for action. During the three critical months, with the client changing mind and bringing in a sub-contractor, progress appears to have been leisurely none of the urgency implied if the premises had to open within four months. The quantum of the counter claim was based on a payback period of which the architect may well have been unaware. The fact that the client appointed another consultant and proceeded to open speedily indicated an urgency not apparent from the file.

Lessons

*   Identify the client.
*   Be aware of the client's objective, timescale and payback period.
*   Be aware that even if the client terminates your appointment, there is always the potential for retrospective claim for loss.

UNEVEN RELATIONSHIP

The situation

The house design had been prepared by a senior architect in a different part of the country. A different architect, having recently set up his new practice, was instructed to provide contract administration and other related services for the construction of the house. Notified of a potential claim for remedial work to a bay and other windows, and to a slate roof, the architect attributes the problems to the builder and the client, and recommends the appointment of an NHBC inspector. The client prefers an independent expert architect (to which the architect agrees reluctantly) to examine the adequacy of the architect's drawings and instructions, the nature of the client's instructions and the quality of the building works.

The expert witness

The bay window had been erected without cavity closers but was not leaking. The water was coming, instead, from defective construction at eaves level. The contractor had used Spanish instead of the specified Welsh slate, and the lead flashings were incorrectly made. He concluded that the architect had lost control of the job. The builder had manipulated the client, thus undermining the architect's authority. There was poor quality building construction. Of the likely remedial costs, the builder should bear 50%, the architect 45% and the client 5%. The architect accepted the expert's comments about construction, but disputed the apportionment of liability. Water ingress was caused by the omission of the original overhanging eaves directly instructed by client to builder, on site, without any reference to him. He bore no liability.

Client and builder instructing the architect on his AIs

Enter the loss adjuster

The architect and his advisers were not prepared to accept 45% liability. It was argued that the expert witness had strayed beyond the original terms of reference (restricted to windows and slates) by examining the eaves. Having done so, he had failed to exhaust his extended terms of reference by examining the liability for the eaves detail and bay window. Client and builder between them had agreed to slice off the original overhanging eaves without reference to the architect. It was accepted that the architect had retrospectively authorised various changes agreed between client and contractor by issuing AIs both in regard to the clipped eaves and the slates, and had failed to spot and have remedied seriously deficient work.

Settlement

After negotiations a final compromise awarded liability of just under 40% against the architect. The builder never disputed the expert's award of 50% of the liability: the net outcome was to increase the percentage awarded against the client.

Lessons

*   The second architect's position was weakened because he was implementing another architect's design without having any commitment to it and thus he did not resist changes proposed by the builder. He allowed his ordinary degree of inspection to be reduced as well as allowing the contractor to propose and carry through design changes. That made it very difficult to compel appropriate remedial works from the contractor.
*   When defects appeared, the client still attacked the architect for failure to use due skill and diligence even where it was the client's own actions in undermining the architect that had led to the failure in the first place.

Moral

If you let your authority as architect slip, and exacerbate that by issuing AIs for alterations of which you did not approve, and have not checked for technical performance, you will end up carrying the can.

NO WINNERS

The architect's progress: the client claiming upon his certificate

The situation

Law suit against one-man band architect for a vast sum encompassing the purchase price of a house, mortgage repayments and loss of interest: on the grounds that the house was collapsing and had no value.

The architect's situation

The largely self-built house was built on a steeply sloping gap site adjacent to the architect's own. The architect had provided drawings and plans, with occasional inspection. The second owner of the house required a certificate to sell it to the pursuer. For reasons of general willingness to help, and neighbourly friends, the architect issued the following certificate: *'I was a supervising architect for the construction of the above dwelling completed ... and I certify that the plans and specification of the building and its construction conform to good building practice with the use of sound materials to the satisfaction of the District Council who granted the Certificate of Completion ...'*

Problems

But the architect was far from being a supervising architect, scarcely involved save for periodic inspection as a neighbour. There was also a danger that the certificate implied a warranty or guarantee, which would have nullified the insurance cover. Worse, the architect did not inspect the property before issuing the certificate.

The claim

The ultimate purchaser bought a broken-backed house, for the trial bores and resulting foundations had been inadequate. The purchaser also sued on the grounds that the settlement cracks in the building were so great as to imply that the certificate constituted fraudulent misrepresentation. If so, the insurance would have been voided (the architect has to act in good faith).

The suit

The pursuer claimed that the house and site were valueless. If the insurance was voided, the architect would be sequestered since the costs were far greater than the assets.

Settlement

In another of these 'imaginative solutions' created by the company's legal adviser, it was decided to underpin the house and put it on the market for resale. The value should be sufficient to repay the purchaser's entire mortgage. Furthermore, the architect would make a substantial personal contribution which would compensate the purchaser for the money he put in, with loss of interest and increase in value. That proved to be the final solution.

Summary

One of the most miserable tales to come before the company. The prime error was that of issuing a certificate from a desire to help where there was no obligation to do so. Secondly, of making an inadequate site investigation on a site whose condition implied that it was advisable. The third error was issuing a certificate the terms of which were close to being unacceptable to the insurance company. The fourth error was to issue the certificate without inspecting the site: which brought the case perilously close to fraudulent misrepresentation.

Lessons

* Skimp site investigation at your peril.
* If you have no responsibility for a site work, do not create the implication that you might have.
* Be wary about issuing any certificates: and never do so without checking the project which the certificate covered.
* Invariably check the wording on the certificate either that it complies with RIAS standard certificates, or that it is acceptable to the insurer.

A MATTER FOR ASTONISHMENT

The situation

The architect pursuing a developer/client for unpaid fees is informed of a likely counterclaim for the costs of design error.

The error

The scheme related to the refurbishment of a post-war housing estate. All dimensions had to be transferred from imperial to metric: which was done by hand within the architect's office. In one instance, the original measurement taken was from the centre of the window to the perimeter; but when it was scaled up, the dimension was taken to represent the entire window. The entire window, however, lit both the living room and the bathroom and under the refurbishment plan, a new slapping would be required to give adequate light to the bathroom, which the contractor did not price since it was not indicated on the drawing.

Negotiations

Despite a large amount of work undertaken by the architect for the developer, the developer sought recovery of the likely oncost (approximately 25% of the outstanding architect's fee) by retention against the fee, rather than lodging a claim. Good existing relationships were likely to be disrupted. The architect agreed with the contractor's estimate of the likely oncost, and its detailed breakdown. The underwriter agreed to recompense the architect for the amount of unpaid fees (less excess) leaving the contractor recompensed for the additional work by his not having to pay the architect's outstanding fees. The condition of the insurance company was that the developer would have to waive any rights to any further claim on the project. A delay of some months in the payment of the settlement occurred because the lawyers did not feel able to pay until a final discharge, on the conditions required by the developer, had been received from them.

Novel development

Within days, the developer had approached the architect again. There had been a change of personnel, and the new broom was concerned at the damage to a long-term relationship for what was a fairly trifling sum. The developer therefore withdrew the claim and settled the outstanding fees. The architect then had to reimburse the insurance company. The condition was that the insurance company withdrew its request for an indemnity against potential further claims.

Lessons

*   This claim arose from a classic error which should not have arisen: but is to easy to make. Although the contractors settled because they felt they had used their economic muscle unfairly against the architects, the architect might well have pursued a defence with a smaller client to the effect that the error in the drawings was so palpable that it could have been picked up by any competent person on site at a sufficiently early stage (even pre-tender if necessary). The decision to settle might therefore be a tacit admission by the developers that they did not want it known that their own highly professional team could not spot a bathroom missing a window when they saw one.
*   Clients are unpredictable.

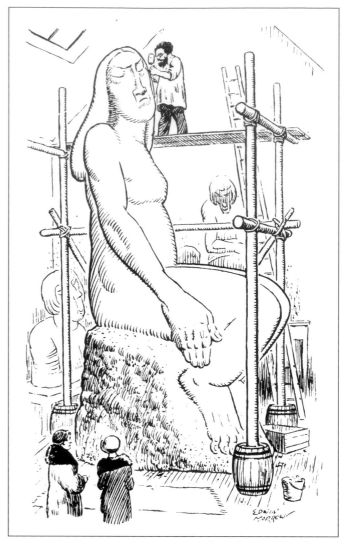

Something awry in scaling-up

A STAIR CASE

Introduction

This sad tale outs how the consequences of inadequate site inspection might lead to an architect's liability for the cost of some of the remedial works. Not unusual, you might think? Well, the significant fact in this instance is that the responsible sub-contractor is still in business.

The situation

A two-storey extension added to the rear of an historic cottage involved alterations to the structure of the staircase. Within about a year, cracking in the ceiling above the staircase had become apparent and there was settlement in adjacent cupboards. The client's engineer recommended immediate propping up with acrow props and an opening up to inspect.

What they discovered

A structural engineer had advised on the structural details relating to the staircase: but during construction, the client requested an alteration to the design. Since it simplified the structure, the architect did not resubmit the drawings to the engineer. He concluded they would not be material. The matter involved a newel post, and the construction of a load-bearing stud partition wall.

The cause

During the contract, the architect had complained several times about the quality of the joinery sub-contractors. Opening up revealed they had not followed the detail of the drawings prepared, nor standard building practice in the construction of the stud partition. Their fixings were wrong, and they had used wrongly sized timber.

The issue of inspection

The architect carried out weekly inspections, which he considered appropriate in normal circumstances given the fee and type of job. However, after much delay, the joiners appeared on site and carried out a substantial amount of work within the space of a week, so by the time of the architect's next visit, the joint and construction details were concealed behind plasterboard.

Complications

The main contractor and the joinery sub-contractor both agreed to return to remedy the work. However, as a consequence of the opening up, the structural engineer required a change to the details, with additional works. These the original contractors refused to accept as being their liability. Consequently, although the problem was one of faulty workmanship, the architect was nonetheless held liable for the cost of those additional works now deemed to be necessary to safeguard the position.

Settlement

The matter was settled thereby. The work undertaken. The client remained supportive and helpful throughout. The architect's insurance bore approximately 50% of the final sum.

Gingerly examining a stair's stability

Lesson

Be aware of what the ordinary competent professional would regard as the critical stages in the building contract i.e. relevant events and take steps to ensure appropriate inspection.

Moral

The replacement of the staircase structure by a new one was clearly a relevant event: and the architect should have been aware that, if he had been worried about the performance of the joiners, he should have been on site during a critical piece of work to check it was being done well enough.

OUCH!

The situation

In the centre of an historic city, adjacent to that city's most famous building, the planning officer notices, one day as he strolls past, that the new building under construction does not conform to what he remembered as the detailed planning permission given to it. On his return to the office he checks the file; and enforces. Work stops.

The issue

For the construction of neo-vernacular flats in a highly sensitive location, the planning authority had stipulated a maximum visual appearance of two-and-a-half storeys which, during construction, appeared to have grown to three full storeys in height at the gables. Although they conformed to the building warrant, they were contrary to the planning permission, and there appeared to be no system, within the district council, of the planners and building control officers cross-checking with each other.

The cause

The planning officer claimed that the wallhead was 1.5m too high, and that the windows and the gable should be a single dormer and not double. The architect admitted that in transfer from planning permission to working drawings, they had wrongly transcribed the size of the wallhead at the gables, but only by 500mm (which the planning officer was later prepared to accept). This difference transferred a two-and-a-half storey building into three. It was put down to inadvertence. Yet, if it was simply inadvertence in the height of the wallhead, how come a single dormer window became translated into a double window? Since the matter of liability was fairly straightforward, the interest in this case lies in the consequence.

The consequence

Work was stopped on site. The building was a timber-kit and the reduction of the wallhead required a fundamental reconsideration including the disposal of already-made components (namely the trusses). The claim began to be built up, comprising time-related loss and expense to the contractor (a majority claim), specific loss and expense, and loss of productivity; and additional finance charges. There was also the potential of a loss claim by the client for increased professional fees and increased finance costs since there would be a delay in completion and then letting. In the outcome, marketing delay proved to be the second largest component of a substantial claim payout.

Lessons

* The sensitivities of the site and the planning permission had clearly been given insufficient priority. Otherwise such palpable variations would never have occurred. In other words, the architect and the planning officer did not share the same visual intention which might have allowed these palpable variations to have been picked up.

'The council says the top ten storeys must come down – some nonsense about controls'

* The drawings submitted for planning permission were incorrectly transcribed and subsequently inadequately checked.
* The architect pleaded that the change was the result of a later attempt to conform to building regulations. If building regulations were to have an impact upon planning matters, they should have been dealt with beforehand.
* It might have been possible for the architect to have picked up the problem before it reached the degree of expense it did; save that the client had employed them solely to obtain planning and building warrant: thereafter moving to design-and-build. Clients who use architects in such a limited manner should be aware of the potential consequences: they forfeit the assistance which their architect can give them once a building begins on site. They probably do not understand it in any case.

Moral

Take planning permissions with the seriousness that planning committees do and stay on the permitted track. Deviations can be disastrously expensive.

PITCHING IT CLOSE

Improbability of copying the adjacent roofs …

This is the sorry saga of an architect who, having made an error or two in design, very nearly ended up paying the full cost of those errors by making much bigger errors once the fault was apparent.

The situation

The roof of a house extension had to match the pitch of its parent which, when the scheme began, had a slated roof. During the three or four years it took the client to decide whether or not to go ahead, he had replaced the slates on the original house with tiles. The roof pitch was so low that the new tiles did not provide an adequate rainwater runoff, which was overcome by putting high performance felt underneath the relevant section of shallow pitch tiles, thus creating a secondary felt roof. Unfortunately, when the extension was resurrected, the architect seemingly failed to check whether the change of material had caused any problem to the parent house. He simply changed the original specified slate to tiles to match.

The consequence

The water ingress, which the contractor had avoided in the original house, materialised in the extension.

The major problems

Perhaps it was because he was not a member of the RIAS (he left that to his partner) but the architect was surely ill-advised. He failed to notify the insurance company, believing that it was a contractor's problem and that the contractor should sort it out. But it was, in fact, a fundamental problem requiring serious work along the lines of the high-performance felt roof in the main house. As soon as the contractor realised what was involved, he refused to do it at his expense. Then the architect made a second error; he admitted liability to the client. Under the policy, admitting liability without the underwriters' consent gives the underwriters the option of voiding the contract. Still failing to perceive the seriousness of the situation, the architect then proceeded to upbraid the insurance company for wasting time, and the loss adjusters for making too much of a meal of it.

Settlement

The loss adjusters, despite all, worked on behalf of the architect. They argued to the underwriters that the failure to notify, and the admission, were not so significant as to constitute unnecessary loss to the underwriters. The policy was not therefore voided. The client possibly under-claimed. Claims for internal redecoration and for legal costs never materialised. The client played a straight bat (albeit an impatient one) since he proceeded to law for the rapid recovery of his outlay for the remedial work to the roof.

Comment

The principal technical lesson is to beware of pulling a scheme out of the drawer, dusting it down and tinkering with it without checking it all through. It is quite possible the architect felt that the change of roofing material from slate to tile was purely cosmetic, but he clearly did not check. There is a dangerous seduction in believing that because something has been done on an existing building, it necessarily works, or can be imitated on a new one.

Lessons

* When asked to proceed on a fairly old scheme, do not dust down: rejuvenate and check.
* If you are matching an existing building, check that the existing building has not changed since you first began designing.
* Notify. You lose nothing by notifying the insurance company, but potentially everything from failing to do so.
* Never commit someone's money without their authority. An admission of liability without the underwriters' permission is doing just that.
* If you have taken two years to notify the insurance company of a circumstance (which might give them the chance of denying the claim), it is perhaps unwise to complain when they take four months to evaluate it.
* As Charon rows you out of Hell, it is not terribly clever to question his seaworthiness.

A RATHER PECULIAR SITUATION

Dangerously impatient to be off

'This is the third time', wrote the exasperated client, *'that we find ourselves on site on one of your contracts without the necessary authorisation'*. A month after the work had begun on the construction of an infill five-storey block of flats, a full building warrant for the scheme as intended had not been received.

The situation

Claims consultants were appointed by the client to investigate cost overrun and a 12-week extension of time on a contract: and, under pressure from Scottish Homes, to seek redress from consultants. They claimed that their clients wished to emphasise that they did not *'raise these matters in a spirit of bitterness or recrimination'*. But it was a troubled contract characterised by delay, casualness and poor communication. The appointment of claims consultants was an almost inevitable consequence of a breakdown of trust (are they paid by the word?).

The claim fell into two parts: first that the architects had failed to provide ventilated lobbies between flats and the stairwell as required for five-storey flats to comply with building regulations. The necessary amendments were made during the contract, when the building was already reaching first-floor level, causing delay and expense to the contractor. Secondly, the engineer had misjudged the size of beams to be installed and had instructed variations directly to the contractor. The delay and expense on this latter point was the larger of the two items.

The architect's case

The architect held that Regulation E25(5) could be variously interpreted, and theirs was justified. Building control had been inexperienced and had led them to believe that their interpretation was correct, since it had not been queried by the time the drawings went out to tender: and the notification of non-compliance was only reached four months later, a week before the contract went on site. Once the problem was known, a temporary building warrant was obtained for the basic works and a mechanical engineer was appointed to design an appropriate mechanical ventilation system. That took three months, and proved to be grossly expensive. Thereafter, five months into the contract, other amendments were made to allow for passive ventilation of the lobbies.

The loss adjuster's position

The loss adjuster did not accept that there was any possibility of a variable interpretation of Regulation E25 and the architect agreed, accepting liability. No liability was attributed to the architect for the problem with the engineer, since the client was taking separate action against the engineers. The matter was eventually settled at a total cost to the architect's insurers and the architect of approximately £18,000.

Important factors

Everybody save the client enjoyed a strange lack of urgency. The architects took almost four months to provide the loss adjuster with sufficient information: and periods exceeding six months sometimes elapsed once matters were referred to the claims consultants. In circumstances where construction work was proceeding without a warrant, the architects nevertheless allowed three months to elapse for the ventilation engineer's proposals, and then blamed the engineer for lack of progress (the responsibility was the architect's). It was perhaps lucky that the client pursued the engineer directly and was happy to leave it at that for delay costs attributable to engineering: because the architect's authority had been called in to question once the engineer instructed the contractor directly (sometimes not informing the architect). The whole sorry saga, however, began with insufficient material being deposited with building control too late for a considered position to be taken before work began on site.

Lessons

* Do not antagonise clients and/or loss adjusters by inefficient or late response.
* The responsibility lies with the architect to submit for building warrant in adequate time for determinations to be given before beginning on site.
* Do not rely on building control to instruct you in the building regulations: know them instead.
* Be more aware of your client's sensitivities and respond to their uncertainties. It is because architects are seen as unresponsive that claims consultants tend to be brought in.

BLOCKBUSTED

A most miserable case, taking eight years to settle (12 years after the first defects were noticed) at quite enormous cost, probably far beyond the value of the building.

Signs of settlement become severe

The situation

A listed building, gutted, was rebuilt internally into four flats: but signs of settlement became so severe that the local authority slapped a dangerous structures notice on it and compelled the four householders to quit and take rented accommodation. The contractor went into liquidation shortly after the preliminary signs of trouble. The occupiers sued for loss of value, cost of remedial work, disruption and consequential loss. The person they sued was a former employee of the original architect who had since set up in practice and had taken on the almost completed project, upon the death of his former employer.

The architect's case

Whilst an employee, he had specified that the central cross-wall should be taken down to the bottom of the original basement as foundation: the basement should be levelled with compacted fill and ground-floor concrete slab laid thereon. The original architect's commission from the developer was that of producing plans, achieving approvals and occasional visits only. It was not a full service and did not involve normal inspection.

The expert witness

The expert witness confirmed what trial excavations had discovered: the central crosswall had not been carried down to the bottom of the basement, but was lying on a ground-floor slab, which was not lying on compacted fill, as instructed, but upon a pile of undulating rubbish from the original building. The expert witness had evil things to say about other aspects of the building construction, transfer of load, sound attenuation and fire retardation, but noted that if the drawings has passed building control, either there must have been a waiver or the extent of poor construction was within tolerable limits. Since the architect's original drawings so far as the cross-wall and the slab were concerned were adequate, he concluded that the primary liability lay with the (liquidated) developers/builders.

Secondary liability

But the second architect had issued a letter, *'to all whom it may concern'*, at the request of the developers, which stated that the (second) architect had been appointed to supervise the construction of the works, and confirmed that, subject to one or two reasonably minor items, the work had been *'completed to a satisfactory standard and in compliance with current building regulations, the approved plans and planning permission'*. But he had been away from the project for a number of months between leaving the firm and his former employer dying. During that period the slab was laid and the crosswall constructed. When the (second) architect came back on to the scene, the ground-floor flat was already carpeted. Yet intending purchasers were offered a full architect's certificate stating that what should have been built had been built properly. Site supervision (a duty no architect should claim to be undertaking) and certification were the two issues.

Outcome

The salient facts of the case were clear early on. It took 6-7 years for the case to progress because all parties allowed it to drag its weary way through the courts before deciding to settle. Settlement, once aggregated by all four properties, would make it one of the most expensive settlements for professional indemnity insurance in Scotland since the inception of the RIAS scheme: and because of an incautious letter relating to a scheme of four wee flats put up by an unreliable developer.

Lessons

* Never claim supervision unless you are specifically appointed and paid to undertake that duty: and are sufficiently frequently on site to be able to undertake it.
* Beware of issuing letters of comfort which assume far more liability than necessary.
* Beware of certifying building work as satisfactory if any stage of that building work has been undertaken without your knowledge or inspection. Blind certification of nine months of uninspected construction proved catastrophic.

Moral

Deploy your signature cautiously and with great circumspection.

WELL BLOW ME DOWN

The situation

An architect receives a telephone call from a fellow architect to inform him that one of his buildings has just collapsed, inviting him to come and have a look. The architect is advised by an eminent lawyer not to go near the place until a formal complaint has been received: which was his second and by far gravest mistake.

The case

A timber-framed sun room sitting on a second-floor roof collapsed, apparently because the main beams supporting the roof of the sun room had become unfixed from the parent building. Down they went, down followed the roof, and the walls swelled outwards. The only option was complete demolition and replacement. Nine months later, a formal complaint was lodged against the architect which focused upon the fixing between the new roof beams and the existing building. From visual inspection of the failed beams, it seemed that the only fixing was manually driven masonry nails joining the new timber beams to existing concrete lintels. They had clearly failed.

The architect's position

The architect pointed out that specification required the fixing to be masonry nails shot-fired into the concrete lintel, rather than manually driven: that both the engineer and building control had been aware of this specification and had not demurred, and that the building had stood up very well for over 10 years without any problems. If the beam had been fixed any other way, that was a matter between the client and the contractor (now in liquidation).

The expert witness

Two of them. The architect expert witness identified three possible methods of fixing a timber beam to a concrete lintel:
a) manually driven nails
b) shot-fired nails; and
c) bolts
He concluded that shot-fired nails would not have taken the stresses or loads, and that bolts were the only competent solution. However, he concluded that the contractor had not followed the specification (the drawings could not be found) and had indeed manually driven them. The engineer expert witness concurred. He found, also, that of the manually driven nails, three had not entered the concrete lintel at all (being bent completely out of shape), and one had totally sheared. For its 10 years life, the sun room had been barely fixed to the parent building, and had stayed erect mainly because of the integrity of its timber frame. It only finally collapsed because of superimposed loading on the roof during repairs. He concurred with the architect that a bolt should have been used.

News of his building's collapse is received with humility:
'Fiddle sticks! Humbug!'

Outcome

The sun room was reinstated by the second architect with a steel frame: and the case was settled expensively: although the architect never accepted the joint expert witness view that shot-fired nails would have been inadequate for the purpose. But they had not been on site at this critical juncture, and had been unable to spot that their instructions had been ignored by the contractor.

Lessons

* At critical stages in a contract, be alert as to whether the contractor is following instructions or not.
* Ensure the engineers are fully aware of structural details and are prepared to underwrite them.

Liability issues

This case almost caused a crisis within the insurance company. The lawyer's advice to the architect not to visit the site, and to take no further action without a formal notification, was wholly wrong. Not only had the architect foregone the opportunity to undertake a personal inspection of the damage and thereby the ability to identify cause; but he failed to notify the insurance company. Although done on the best advice, the company denied liability on the grounds of late notification. The company was then new, and the RIAS had agreed with underwriters an *'Innocent non disclosure clause'*. The company chairman threatened to resign unless the company was prepared to undertake this case. After some hard bargaining, it relented, did take on the case but at a substantial excess. It proved to be very expensive indeed for both.

Professional lessons

* If your building collapses, notify your insurer immediately.
* Ask your insurer's permission to visit the site so that you can make proper records which could prove vital to your position in any subsequent law case.

AN EXPENSIVE COST-SAVING

The situation

A third of the way through the contract to build old people's housing in a conservation area, the planning officer issued a stop notice on the grounds that artificial stone was being used on the façade, whereas the permission had been for natural stone. It was admitted immediately that the drawings had stated natural stone and that, therefore, the planning officer was correct.

The error

The architect claimed that his client could never have afforded stone and had never authorised the use of 'natural stone' on the drawings. Those words had been added by the firm's technician and had remained undetected. Worse, the discrepancy between the drawings stating natural stone and the later specification and bills specifying artificial stone seemed not to have been spotted either.

Plea for retrospective permission

In many respects the design was comparable to buildings with comparable materials just further west, and elsewhere in the city. The fact that conservation-area designation had been imposed retrospectively should not have added further onerous burdens to the client, a charitable institution dependent upon public money. There was never any intention to deceive as the army of 'conservationalists' [sic] claimed. It was a simple error whose gravity had been compounded by the later designation as a conservation area. Had they known about an *a priori* requirement for real stone for the façade, the probability is that the client would not have bought the site in the first instance. The sheltered accommodation was providing a much-valued service in that district; were the client to withdraw entirely, the city would be disadvantaged. The arguments put forward to the planning subcommittee for retrospective permission were unsuccessful; as they were before the full planning committee, whose members were subject to considerable lobbying from both the client and the 'conservationalists'.

What to do next?

The client concluded that the project was too far through to abandon. In view of the fact that the architect had admitted liability (albeit it blaming a technician) they decided to seek recompense from him.

Calculation of costs

The legal and loss adjuster costs were not insignificant. Second, the additional costs of using real stone with stonemasons came to over £80,000. The third cost was the contractor's claim for delay. Delays in identifying the right stone with the right stonemasons put the contractor substantially behind schedule. The final cost element – namely the client's original proposal to sue for interest and loss of beneficial use of the building – was not pursued. Even so, the losses went well into six figures.

The technician decides to apply natural stone

Analysis

The final cost was almost three times the reserve. Six months elapsed between the notification and the final decision to proceed with natural stone. The focus on trying to persuade the council to change its mind took the team's eye off the ball, and reduced the urgency of trying to find the most economic stone for erection in the speediest manner. Although it was, ultimately, the architect's insurance that paid all costs of delay to the contractor, client, underwriters, lawyers and loss adjusters, all contributed to that delay possibly because the architect was inadequately decisive.

Lessons

* Although not a factor in this case, beware (if ever you are tempted to help your client in this way) of trying to circumvent planning legislation in the hope they might not notice. The costs are truly horrendous.
* The façade of a project, and the specification of its materials, is essential to the building's integrity. Even if it is detailed by a technician, the responsibility is the architect's and should be checked.
* The specification, or bill (as appropriate) should correlate with the drawings. Discrepancies should be identified and resolved.
* If ever caught in such a trap, prepare for the worst, and have an appropriate plan ready for operation as fast as possible. When a contract is already running, every second counts.

CLUBBED TO DEATH

The architects remained disinclined to hurry to the site ...

The situation

Within nine years of completion, conditions in a club had got so bad that a survey was called for. It revealed cracks in the parapet, a dying felt roof, substantial evidence of damp and condensation on the ceiling, dripping from the roof-lights disfiguring the timber floor below. Damp problems, condensation problems and a number of sundry minor items demonstrated a lack of routine maintenance. The client, anxious to avoid litigation, invited the architects to return to prepare drawings and specification for remedial work, without charge. The architects offered unspecified services from a retired partner, but otherwise would not comply with the suggestion. They denied liability.

The next step

Eight months later, no further action had been taken, and the decay was accelerating. The architects remained unwilling to assist since no specific or proved errors had been substantiated against them. Exasperated, the client appointed other architects to undertake remedial works, which would form the basis of a negligence claim. The work, which included the discovery and eradication of dry rot, and the construction of a new pitched roof, totalled over £70,000: much of which was, according to the second architects, attributable to the parapet detailing.

Enter the loss adjuster

The loss adjuster's primary interest lay in the possibility that the case was time-barred, in that the damage was either discovered or was reasonably discoverable over five years before the claim had been lodged. That this defence was dropped hinged on the fact that, whereas some damp symptoms had clearly been evident from early on, it would be difficult if not impossible to demonstrate that those symptoms could have been attributed to the fault that was eventually discovered, rather than to condensation, poor use of the central heating system or lack of maintenance.

Enter the expert witness

Since the remedial work had been completed, the expert witness did not visit the site, but judged upon documents and drawings. The architects' intransigence to accept involvement meant that they had deprived themselves or their advisers of the opportunity for personal inspection on site. The long litany of problems were resolved into four possible groups: first the problems caused by the club abandoning the heating system and using Calor gas, thus increasing condensation; second, botched remedial repairs; third, complaints that were not in themselves significant (e.g. no damp-proof course under a urinal stall base); and finally, the one substantive complaint which was probably the cause of all the remainder of the problems: namely a defective wall-parapet detail.

The designer had opted for a solid parapet, which he had thickened to 225mm; and had not followed CP121. He had, in the words of the expert witness, *'not understood that most of the water penetrates the joints and not the bricks, and merely increasing the thickness of the wall would only have marginal benefit'*. Furthermore, the damp-proof course did not extend to the full width of the wall. Roof joints and ceiling support timbers adjacent to the external wall became saturated. Finally, concrete bricks had been used ignoring the extent to which they were susceptible to long-term irreversible shrinkage.

Outcome

The case was restricted to the consequences of the faulty parapet detail and settled at approximately 50% of the total cost.

Lessons

* Failure by the architects, despite encouragement by the insurers, to become involved in remedial work and assist the client, terminated to their disadvantage.
* The junction between wall and roof, particularly in Scotland, is a traditionally vulnerable spot; and any departure from the Code of Practice should be a deliberate rather than accidental decision, supported by up-to-date information.
* A small design error had major consequences for the entire building project.
* It is an unwise architect who assumes his client will necessarily undertake the maintenance and management that he envisages.

INFLATED

The architect made commercial assumptions that could not be sustained

The situation

In early 1990, the recession barely lapping Scotland, an architect valued five commercial properties in seeming full swing. In 1994, the architect dead, his firm in voluntary liquidation, the building society sued for gross overvaluation of five derelict, unlet units over which they held mortgages. The extent of claim lies in the top 10 of RIASIS wheeze bangers.

The case

The building society had commissioned a surveyor to value the properties as they might have been in 1990, lest the high resale price was a cause of the continuing lack of sale. He had concluded with values from 20% to 60% lower than the architect's. He had also observed imprecision in the architect's valuation (did they include goodwill or not? Did they include assumptions about level of trade or not?).

The defence

The insurance company, on behalf of the legatees, commissioned a further valuation survey. The second surveyor concluded that the architect had indeed grossly overvalued, but that the sum claimed was far too high in respect of two matters:

a) The building society had seen the trading figures of each operation and should have made up its own mind, and not relied upon the architect's vacuous comments such as: *'Whilst we were not able to examine trading records, from observation it was obvious that a good trading pattern exists and income should reflect this'*. In stating this, the architect had gone not just beyond his competence, but beyond any evidence into speculation.

b) The building society manager was well aware that the architect was not a qualified valuation surveyor. Contributory negligence of 15% was accepted by the building society.

The surveys

A comparison of the architect's optimistic and the surveyor's pessimistic surveys of the properties is instructive:

Architect	Surveyor
very active trading area	local economy struggling to recover from major mine closures
bituminous felt roof appears in good condition	inferior form of roof construction with short life expectancy
a very viable shopping unit	irregular shape and layout

The above are good examples of the difference between the two. The surveyor's valuation is precise in its exclusions, in drawing attention to legislation, to likely changes and to past changes. The architect's surveys, which indeed include detailed measurement (lacking in the surveyor's) generally comprise the description of the buildings as they appeared. There are further differences in spotting rotting windows, cracking roofs or boss harl: but these may have been the consequences of the four-year gap between the two.

Principal lesson

The primary lesson derives from the distinction between the two types of survey. The valuation survey is focused upon the future use of the property: what needs to be changed, what might have to be changed and what might inhibit use (e.g. a windowless room). The architect's survey is a building survey with measurement which makes assumptions about condition but does not address further use changes whatsoever.

Conclusion

The surveys took the architect far beyond his competence into assumptions that could not be sustained. The result was horrendously expensive (not including the failure of traders who were having to carry too high a mortgage).

Moral

If you are going to diversify beyond architecture, you must do it competently. Understand the rules and demands of the new field into which you are entering and answer the question that is being asked of you (and not the question you wanted to be asked).

PS: of interest is that the claim was covered by a past liability/runoff policy effected by the architect's widow, the legatee to the architect's estate. In the absence of the professional indemnity policy, the architect's estate would have been responsible for payment of the claim monies due. In addition, the expert advisers employed by the insurers succeeded in reducing the original sums claimed significantly – an outcome which may not have been achieved by the widow defending the claim without the support of professional indemnity insurers.

SQUASHED

The situation

The builder sued the client for non-payment of a certificate and for additional works on two squash courts. The client counterclaimed on grounds of damp, poor workmanship and increased cost. The case hinged upon the architect.

The case

The client desired a quality job. He decided to do the finishes himself, but kept hiking the specification: iron balustrades, for example, replaced with marble. The context of the claim was that, for such reasons, the original costs had been exceeded by over £30,000. However, the squash courts were finished too late for the season, there appeared to be damp at floor level, mould on the walls and some poor quality finishes for which the builder was responsible.

The issue

The dpc had been laid a course too high, at the level of the timber floor rather than the concrete solum below. Worse, the dpc overlap had been ripped during construction, the tears leading back into the wall structure. Finally, it transpired that the wall cavity had been so filled with rubbish that it was acting as a damp bridge.

The case against the architect

First, although the architect knew that the dpc was too high, he did not instruct its redoing. Second, someone – perhaps architect, perhaps builder (they each claimed the other) – asked BRE what to do about the ripped membrane. A reluctant answer was to inject surrounding silicone by an approved contractor. Silicone was injected, not by an approved contractor, and it did not work. It was not clear whether the architect had either instructed this work or had approved it. Finally, the architect had issued a certificate of practical completion in the face of damp and client complaint (which he appears later to have withdrawn). That certificate would have removed liability from contractor to architect.

Progress of the case

The arbitration between contractor and client was settled by a small payment by builder to client (i.e. a substantial acceptance of the client counterclaim). The client then claimed against the architect for breach of duty (as above). A new expert witness found only local damp, easily remediable, the mould and fungus dry and historic, and therefore not a great case. The client sued for £100,000 (in addition to the substantial sum received through the non-payment of certificate and the settlement), building up a case on grief, time spent, lawyer's fees and much else beside.

Settlement

A low four-figure sum was offered, more than sufficient to deal with the outstanding damp problem, and the matter was concluded.

'The client decided to replace iron with marble, and to select the finishes himself'

Lessons

* Much was made over the architect's inspection duties (counsel insisted on the word supervision, and reliance on old law). The laying of that dpc was clearly a relevant event requiring attendance, and the architect's decision not to enforce a re-doing at the correct level made him weak. After all, if his original design had been correct, why was he happy to accept a material change?
* A major weakness, lay in the lack of control over the remedial action: who specified, who instructed and who approved.
* The final straw was the issue of the practical completion certificate in the knowledge of client unhappiness over mould and damp.

Morals

* Hope (that something will work) is no substitute for firm direction based on knowledge; if in doubt, consider taking senior advice.
* Remember that the practical completion certificate transfers significant patent (i.e. easily observable or visible) quality issues from builder to architect.

RAIN STOPPED PLAY

'Don't let that fall on the opening ceremony, George'

The situation

Sufficient water penetration through the roof of a multiplex cinema caused a ceiling to collapse after some two years of remedial work. The client sued the architect for a handsome six-figure sum; and separately planned to tackle the builder in arbitration. That it was finally settled at two thirds of the sum sued for indicated that their beef was justified, but not in the way they originally targeted.

Nice work

The multiplex client had sold on twice; the first builder had been deeply unimpressive. After severe programme slippage (it was a building whose formal opening date was fixed prior to letting the contract), the contractor flooded the site with brickies. Later evidence was to show horribly blocked cavities and damaged pre-formed metal deck roofing. However, he was a friend of the client (which ultimately proved useful). It more or less leaked from the day of the first showing; but the remedial builder was even worse, and went into liquidation.

The claim

The architect was alleged to have been negligent in the design of the coping, the fixings and parapet gutters, a roof wrongly specified in terms of insulation and insufficiently strong for its purpose, and failure to provide adequate access to roof machinery. Further, he had failed to spot inadequate cavity trays and other bad workmanship. By issuing a certificate of practical completion whilst there was outstanding works, he had transferred builder's liability to himself. He was also held liable for faulty design and inspection of the remedial works.

The defence

The client had insisted upon occupation of the complex on a date when he knew that the architect's reservations about the roof had not been satisfied. The architect had no choice but to issue the certificate, although he had waited six months and then back dated it. The reduction in specification of the roof had been at the client's insistence in order to reduce costs: but, in any case, should have been sufficient for the purpose. The design of copes was a matter for the domestic sub-contractor, and no liability attached to the architect. As for the cavity trays, there was no longer any evidence to prove one way or the other: but the architect's records showed more than sufficient attendance on site, and more than sufficient instruction to the first, then the second builder, as to remedying defects.

Progress of the case

Although the architect served a contribution notice on the first builder joining them to the action, the architect's counsel concluded his exposure to be 25% for cavity trays, skirtings and damaged roof on grounds of inadequate inspection: the balance to the builder 50% for parapet, since the domestics had submitted drawings to the architect who had made no comment (i.e. potentially deemed approval) and 100% of additional costs of providing access to machinery on roof. They were also thought liable for 100% of the remedial works (save that there was a substantial retention to offset). Marginally, at first, but eventually to two-thirds percentage, the first builder accepted principal liability, and the case was duly settled.

Lessons

* Although the architect was covered for each and every claim, his excess was claimed for each: three in this case.
* Because it was settled, the issue of the practical completion certificate was never tested: nor was the possibility of contributory negligence by the client.
* The contract used was evidently at odds with the client's irreversible time scale.
* The architect was unwise to believe that nobody would ever require access to the roof; and even more so not to insist on duckboards during construction if it was as likely to prove as fragile as it did.

Morals

* Make sure the contract is appropriate to the task in hand.
* Beware of deemed acceptance of drawings by others.
* Minimise liability for 'inadequate' inspection by maintaining methodical records. PCC has nothing to do with politically correct: it stands for the perils of completion certificate.

TAKEN FOR GRANTED

The situation

What if, by virtue of an architect's alleged delay in completion, the value of a flat fell far below the money spent on its rehabilitation? Worse, what if that spend had been overspend, justified on grounds of optimistic sale price? Worse still, what if the architect had claimed to 'supervise' dry rot specialists who undertook an inadequate job, leaving more rot to be uncovered by prospective purchasers' surveyors? Indeed, who also discovered a delicate sewage smell? Answer: the architect pursued by the demons of hell for everything from the additional costs, to the redoing of rot work, to the difference in property values: all in all, for a lot of bananas.

Context

Not far from a no-win situation. A tiny commission to the architect for a minor upgrade of a tenement within a block within an area in the process of uncompleted and staggered upgrading. *'Whoopee'*, says he: *'go for a grant'*. Unfortunately, the local authority required much more than the client really wished. To get the grant, the contract sum trebled. Local authority required specialist work not forecast by architect: full bill of quantities, and, during the contract, timber treatment etc. But prices were going up and the area was going up. The client was assured reluctantly that her net outlay would remain constant for a vast increase in useful work. Ho hum.

The scheme unravels

The local authority will not release grant money until remedial work to damp, rot and smell is complete. The client cannot pay the architect's certificate without grant money. The flat stalls. It is put on a market which is declining. The area is not improving as fast as forecast. Purchasers discover smells.

The issues

The client held the architect liable for not identifying rot in the first instance, at the point of the initial small contract, which meant that work began prior to eradication. Secondly, the 'supervision' of rot treatment was inadequate, since it had to be redone. Third, both rot treatment and main contracting work had been certified as complete when it was not. Finally, the architect had advised the client to spend more on the property than the surrounding area could sustain.

Settlement

A relatively small settlement (25% of the total claim) was achieved, based solely upon the additional contract costs, ignoring the fall in property value and loss and inconvenience. However, it was cash in hand for the pursuer, and avoided some of the more difficult issues being tried in court (where the architect might have been vulnerable).

Egregious over-enthusiasm at the client's brief

Lessons

* The rot issue could have been argued as latent rather than patent, but the inadequacy of the works when undertaken lay partly with the architect who certified it.
* By certifying as adequate work that which the grant authority declared inadequate, the architect put himself and the client gravely at risk. A discussion with the grant officer prior to certification might have avoided the problem.

Morals

* Beware of over optimism on your client's behalf.
* However small the job, survey carefully.
* Don't supervise: inspect.
* Certify with care; and only when you are satisfied that you are happy taking onto your shoulders what hitherto, in the contract, had been upon the builder's.
* Beware of the Greeks even bearing gifts; grant aid can be as much a curse as a benefit.

BAD AMENITY

The situation

When does a client lose confidence in the architect? Depends upon the scale of the problem and the sophistication of the client. An uncertain client can lose confidence at an architect's first error no matter how large. In this case, mainly because the officials seemed uncertain how to handle the architect's mistake, they hid behind aggressive reports to committee; and the latter, having no other knowledge, had to believe what they were told. Despite the architect's extremely prompt remedial action to rectify an acknowledged error, there was a complete (and probably unnecessary) deterioration in the relationship between client and architect.

The occasion

The case of the muddied brief. The site was part of a much larger development site, and originally to hold, *inter alia*, a warden's house, etc. It was then changed to provide for specialist elderly housing. Two years later, the project was revived.

The new situation

All kinds of problems coincided. First, the client's timescale was accelerated. Second, the brief changed to the less expensive amenity housing without a warden's house. Third, the architect's partnership was breaking up, putting someone new in charge of a fast project.

The case

The new partner did not realise/was not informed that the housing was to be to amenity standard, and substantially different from the rest of the site. All housing and fitments within were provided to mainstream standards: absence of handrails, baths at the wrong height, switches at the wrong height, etc. A fairly costly matter.

The issue

Upon practical completion, the client instructed the architect to make the necessary alterations, stating that they would be held liable for the additional works. The architects, whilst carrying out the works, pointed out that at no time during the contract had the clients commented upon the drawings, nor indeed upon the building as it progressed. Although they did not say so, they were puzzled that, retrospectively, they were being pursued to undertake things to which they assumed the client had given passive but tacit approval.

Outcome

The architects were held liable to the whole costs of remedial action, and the insurers paid it, less the excess. Client/architect relations were strained; partner/former partner relations very much more strained (the excess had to form part of the breakup settlement).

Just not quite wide enough

Lessons

* Project record keeping must be meticulous: particularly in identifying and recording all salient aspects of a project's brief and the categories of accommodation.
* Periodic cross-checking of the project's development with the final agreed brief is valuable.
* Do not assume absence of client reaction is tacit approval unless your correspondence explicitly states that. The responsibility remains yours; and the extent to which any future liability can be modified by contributory negligence by the client is very uncertain.

Moral

The real moral is about the client. People do make mistakes, and are covered for them. Their quality generally shows in their speed and efficiency in remedying them (in this case good). This case need not (should not?) have followed the route it did. How come the client was held exempt from contributory negligence? The act of omission was that of the architect; but could not the client have been deemed to be an expert client; have spotted the error in the drawings, and again have spotted the omissions during construction? The answer, probably, is that the client was not expert enough: and that the aggressiveness shown by the officials was partly due to a feeling of vulnerability in that they had not spotted the errors as they had occurred.

TOTAL DISASTER

An architect's attempt to identify his client misfires

Introit

Join me in a small job; a wee job for the chaps next door. Poor fellows – four residents and two commercial proprietors have received a repairs notice: common repairs to chimney-heads, gable etc. Nothing to worry about: four-figure sum, not worth separate bank account, client meetings etc. Let's just get it done, eh? Why bother with formal client structure etc? (Well, if you had, you wouldn't be here, would you?)

Contract

Two tenders: one 350% higher than the other. Lower tender taken to council for grant purposes: awarded, and contract begins. Should only be months. (Query: why was the difference in the tenders not checked out?)

Contract runs slow and poorly. Client dissatisfaction appears to grow. In the meantime, more work is required to be done: quite a lot more work: approximately 350% more work. (Contractors later to claim that they had never seen the repairs notice; only the architect's limited documentation. Had they seen it, they would have submitted a tender far more like their competitor.) Clients are not informed about the new work and additional grant is not applied for. Two commercial clients are not even included in the original client group. Work is eventually complete, final certificate applied for and agreed, to a sum 350% above agreed contract and grant availability.

Nemesis

Clients refuse to accept certificate and pay final bill. Contractors sue architect as employer. Architect now in Catch 22: as agent, did he have sufficient authority to commit the additional work; and, if so, had he done it competently and in his clients' best interests (i.e. beginning work prior to grant approval)? Secondly, had he defined his status as agent of the clients adequately to the contractors?

Redefinition of the status of clients' agent

The sheriff was told that the contractors had been informed three times that the architect was acting on behalf of clients. But the documents in question stated; (1) The owners of . . . (2) The residents of . . . (3) The proprietors of . . . . They were not specified by name. Each of the above designations implied something different, did not necessarily imply heritable proprietor, and did not clarify whether another party had a charge over the premises. He held that *'it was far from clear that the principals had been adequately identified'*, and that since *'there was no adequate identification of the principals'*, the architect had contracted as agent for an undisclosed principal, and was, therefore, personally liable for the contract.

Awful complication

An architect being sued for debt by a contractor is not covered by PII: the policy only covers the consequence of a negligent act by the architect on behalf of clients. Initially, RIASIS refused to cover the architect.

Outcome

Enter RIASIS negotiating team. First, it persuaded the insurers to change their mind when it realised the potential underlying threat of claims from the clients of negligence in running the contract (the reason why the clients had not honoured the certificate in the first place). Second, it persuaded the contractors to accept a settlement whereby the insurers (with architect's excess) would pay the contractors the amount of grant that should have been applied for (around two thirds of the sum sued) and at the insurers' expense, pursue the clients for their contribution for their percentage of the additional sum to go directly to the contractors.

Lessons

*   Identify your client to the contractor. If you do not, you may be held personally liable.
*   Never, never treat a commission in a manner as cavalier as this no matter how small, no matter whether neighbours: so, always:
    – establish proper client identification;
    – establish proper client committee/group;
    – establish a separate bank account;
    – consult the client on works and variations;
    – seek grants on your client's behalf;
    – never spend your client's money without prior authorisation.

THE THICK FELT LINE

An angry neighbour never sleeps

Introduction

The case of the enraged neighbour, the kit builder, the drawings-only architect and his self-employed associate ended in compensation for the client: at 30 times the fee he had paid the architect. Not bad, since he had originally been hunting for compensation over 60 times his architect's fee.

The case

The architect was employed at minuscule fee by a repeating kit-building client to prepare a site layout of speculative houses for planning permission. An unenthusiastic neighbour, keenly scrutinising its manifestation on site, spotted that two houses were not as planning permitted, but had crept too close. He went public on the matter: it hit the broadsheets, and the council was persuaded to enforce. Retrospective permission was refused, so the case went to appeal. Work on the two houses ceased for 18 months.

The cause

The architect's self-employed associate had been put in charge of this unremunerative and unexciting task. He laid out the scheme on an undimensioned 1:500 draft title plan, whose boundary was defined by a thick felt pen. Unfortunately, he took the outside edge of the felt-tip as the boundary, whereas it was the inner one. On site, the difference came to 1.2 metres, and one of the houses was 800mm offside. Oh what an eagle eye had that neighbour! The architect had been provided with a fully detailed site plan, but seems not to have used it.

Contributing parties

The client had a site engineer. Anyway, the architect's limited commission had prevented him from checking the layout on site. He claimed that, therefore, the site engineer and the client had themselves taken responsibility for accuracy on site at least to the level of contributory negligence. The loss adjuster held, however, that the responsibility lay with the architect since the client was compelled to build according to the plan that had obtained planning permission, and that the site engineer did not have a duty in that respect.

First result

Big sigh of relief. Appeal granted, houses completed and sold: surely case over?

The next step

The repeating 'friendly' client sues for loss and expenses. After much negotiation, a very large sum is agreed (30 times the architect's fee) which broke down as follows: 30% on interest charges; 25% loss on resale; 18% legal fees; 9% additional construction costs; 5% planning fees: and the rest a miscellany of costs including compensation for client time.

The ironic result

The self-employed associate sets up on his own, taking the client.

Lessons

* Responsibility may attach to the slightest act, and even more to planning permission documentation: so do it carefully.
* An angry neighbour never sleeps.
* Never assume: check, cross reference and use all relevant documentation.
* However self-employed (and neither RIBA nor RIAS approve), an associate may commit the firm.
* A thick line should not imply a thick head.

Moral

Consider the huge liability resulting from a piffling fee for an ignominious commission accepted only to please a repeating client who sues then dumps you. Loyalty was a one-way street.

CHEAP

Girls behaving badly

Beware of the privately funded school. Many, as those who know some prominent Edinburgh schools are only too well aware, seem to have abandoned the quality levels achieved by their predecessors.

The situation

The floor of a new girls' shower room remained submerged more than anticipated. The installation of a new gully helped little, and an expert witness, summoned to examine cracks in the cubicles, in the tiles and between tiles and shower trays, uncovered a soggy disaster requiring wholesale replacement of floor.

The cause

As the tail end of a much larger project, the client desired the installation of a girls' shower room within an existing gym. The architect's proposal to install a new concrete floor with ceramic tiles was rejected as unnecessarily expensive . He had to make use of an existing tongue and groove timber floor, at a level that barely gave any fall at all. Once the concrete had been rejected both as floor and between the shower trays, it seems that he left the specification of the new substitute to the contractor, specifying only that the surface should be sealed vinyl; and that the behaviour of the girls in the shower should be carefully regulated.

Sadly, the *'careful supervision of the use of the showers'* proved a vain hope. Had he never read St Trinian's? Girls simply would not close their shower cubicle curtains. Moreover, the janitor had, periodically, to hose the shower trays out. The floor spent much of its time flooded. Water seeped beneath the vinyl, and the floor beneath moved. Tiles cracked, sealant moved, and more water penetrated.

When the expert witness took it all up, he found that the contractor had used timber between the shower trays, and chipboard for a secondary floor. There was wet rot, and the chipboard had dissolved into hominy grits.

The architect's position

The architect claimed that the client was aware that it was a cheap, second best floor, and that the use of chipboard was a matter *'properly left within the design responsibility of the contractor'*, whose installation (he accepted it as wrong anywhere near moisture) would have been imperceptible to reasonable visual inspection.

Pleadings

Whatever the client pressure, the decision was the architect's. Settlement prevented the court examining whether it was proper for the architect to leave the floor specification to the contractor. It seems unwise. However, although the client sued for the entire five-figure cost of replacement by a proper concrete floor, it was held that the client would always have had to pay for that: and that the damage was limited to the original cost of the cheap floor and remedial action; less than half the total amount.

Lessons

* The architect specifies and takes responsibility, regardless of client pressure, unless a written acceptance of the risks is issued by the client.
* The architect believed that the cheap compromise would work. They rarely do.
* The architect abdicated responsibility for the specification of critical floor elements: but had to accept liability for them.
* A design that will only work where people (particularly girls) are constrained to act unnaturally, is likely to have a limited useful life.

OVER THE TOP

Just a bit too hot for comfort

Imagine mainland West Highlands – the damp, the wet and the midges. Imagine therefore, in a locality principally of tourists and salmon fishers, being invited to design four family cottages and six bungalows for a housing association. Surely a wee bit of over specification might help the blighters and nobody would notice?

The issue

Somebody did: the single radiator in the house became so hot it almost scalded a child; and in the works to install radiator guards, the plumbers noticed that the polypropylene feed and expansion tank had become deformed and distorted by boiling water and steam, concluding that the hot water cylinder and entire pipework were at risk.

The cause

Since electricity supply was intermittent, the client wished for primary heating to be by storage heaters, supplemented by a solid fuel fire, back boiler, immersion heater, with one single radiator from the back boiler as heat sink. The boiler unit specified had the capacity for the entire central heating system including hot water, not simply one radiator. The result was that its operating temperature created the risk of scalding.

Specification

There were alternative, appropriate specifications which were rejected. The architect had a hazy recollection that the unit was one recommended or required by the client, but no formal minutes of client meetings existed. The architect specified, the contractor installed as specified, and the responsibility lay with the architect.

Remedy

All dwellings were occupied, furnished and decorated. To replace the boilers would have entailed serious disruption, and would have been the most expensive course of action. It was decided to use the system as it was really designed; replacing the storage heaters with a full central heating system from the back boiler, appropriate to the unit's capacity.

Lessons

* Record client decisions carefully, else you end up paying for them.
* Specification is the duty of the architect.
* Specification is an exact science. Over specification is neither just being cautious; nor even being kind. It can result in something not being appropriate to its function. Both architects and children can get scalded.

MUCH ADO ABOUT NOTHING

The situation

Dry rot spread throughout an elderly school sports pavilion after its conversion to include showers. It proved very expensive to eradicate, and the client sought to fix the blame on the building team. The architect denied liability so the client, without any discussion, proceeded direct to writ. Truly something must have been chewing his armpits.

The claim

An expert witness considered there was a casual link between increased moisture form the showers and the rot. The client threw the book at the architect claiming negligence: in that there was insufficient extraction; in that spillage and splashing from showers had not been anticipated or coped with; in that there were air inlets below ground level attracting water; in the failure to ensure the contractors built to specification; and particularly in the failure to reject the service engineer's proposal to install ventilator grilles in the ceiling.

The riposte

Dry rot was probably latent in the building anyway. So the architect had three lines of defence, in order of credibility: a) workmanship: the client had his own clerk of works on site, who spotted nothing. The problems of lino, adhesive and dpc could not have been spotted by reasonable visual inspection; b) the below-floor level ventilators were pre-existing; and it was not for the architect to challenge the M & E engineer. No evidence had been forthcoming that either was a cause of the rot; c) the client had demanded minimum intervention and least cost which was why, with the client's agreement, they had not included mechanical ventilation.

The issue

But, technically, should they have? Since the case never came to court, any architect liability for the services engineer was never tested. But in relation to the use of the building, their own defence that any additional moisture would be dispersed by opening the windows was weak. The tiles and linoleum were penetrated because ground staff hosed down the showers. If that had not been forecast, when were they last in a changing room shower? Second, they were nonplussed that schoolboys would persist in their refusal to open the shower windows or, worse, would close them when staff had opened them. The lawyer was underwhelmed: *'A court would be slow to be impressed by an argument that schoolboys in Scotland in January would be expected to shower in rooms with windows wide open'.*

Outcome

The client settled for no damages and no costs, provided the architect waived outstanding fees.

A court would be underwhelmed by people compelled to endure discomfort

Lessons

* Watch lest the knock-on effect of changes in environmental conditions in one part of a building does not cause trouble elsewhere.
* Be clear about the division of responsibility between you and other consultants.
* The presence of a client's clerk of works was critical in testing whether builder work was passable.

Moral

It is false economy to construct a building which can only work if the occupants behave unnaturally. Showering in January winds takes Calvinism a mite too far.

SHOP WITH CARE

Beware of straying beyond your knowledge

The situation

Client sues builder and architect: builder for being 18 months behind programme and scheme being badly built; builder and architect for encroachment; and architect for wrongly advising on damages. The sums are large.

The claim

An inner-city shopping street with a difficult, irregularly-shaped site with shaky shops which the client decides to rebuild. The contractor is inefficient and the contract late but, with the agreement of the client (since it was cheaper), there are no L & A damages. But the way it is done appears to preclude the client's rights in common law.

So the client determines to sell the shops and has a buyer, only to find a marginal encroachment on adjacent land prevents the sale. The land is bought, a new purchaser found, but is prepared only to pay considerably less. In the meantime, the client has to fund the capital. So he sues for the cost of the adjacent land, the difference in sale price, the cost of funding the additional time and for the common law damages he would have sued the contractor for.

Issue one: L & A damages

To keep costs down, the contract had no L & A damages. The method chosen was by the architect entering 'nil' in the contract. An English case Temloc vs Erroll had concluded that 'nil' also removed the client's right in common law to sue for poor performance. The issue had not been tested in Scotland. (Still not. This item was withdrawn, the client settling separately with the contractor.)

Issue two: Encroachment

The building encroached to a maximum of 0.3 metres to the rear. The architect claims the drawings were correct: the contractor held that setting out was not his responsibility. Both blamed the structural engineer who had primary duty to identify foundations in view of the proximity to adjacent buildings. The client held that setting out lay within the architect's broader duty of care.

Enter the sheriff

Pity the client. In most instances, the sheriff held that the pleadings were insufficient and that, even where a case could have been made, insufficient evidence was forthcoming to make it. The sheriff found: a) the client had failed to demonstrate that a failure to inspect was relevant to the issue, or had been proved; b) the client had put forward insufficient evidence to demonstrate culpability in the architect's failure to monitor the setting out but he held it a relevant issue, particularly in a difficult site involving demolition; c) that since the issue of funding costs had emerged since the architect's appointment, it was not relevant; d) that the drawings might have been in error should be tested in court.

Result

Case closed with no damages, each party bearing own costs.

Lessons

* Don't alter the contract without professional advice.
* Have a care re: L & A damages, and check with a lawyer.
* Architect may have a duty of care to check setting out particularly in difficult sites.
* Consequential loss might well be a charge against the architect if it were a condition of the commission.

Moral

Retain control of the contract.

A RELEVANT EVENT

Operational difficulties for a café caused by water leaking through the roof; and the proprietor's inspired fin-de-siècle response …

The situation

Seven years after occupation, a café suffers water ingress from the roof; not for the first time but for the first time since the main contractor went bust. The architects claimed that the contractor had not built to specification; but since he could no longer be pursued, the architects seemed to the client a likely substitute. But that wasn't the entire story anyway.

The issue

The leaks were traced to lead-covered dormer windows and ventilators, and associated valley gutters. There was a question whether the gutters were wide enough, given the rainfall and pine needles, and whether the Code 4 lead was strong enough in the exposed climate. The critical issue, however, was the architects' instruction to the builder that all flashing and associated details were to be in accordance with the relevant codes of practice of the Lead Development Association. On inspection, they were not. The builder had welded the lead rather than having it folded and clipped. There was thus no provision for expansion, and it had failed.

The loss adjuster

The principal reason why liability attached to the architects was not that they were carrying the contractor's liability; but that they had certified the work. Why had the variation not been spotted on inspection? The loss adjuster noted several contingent points: first, the detail was in the hands of a technician; second, the detailed drawings of the dormers were not ready at the point of contract, but were issued during the course of the works; finally, there was no record of any specific site inspection with regard to the dormer leadwork.

Settlement

The cost was considerable, but the client settled at 30% less for three reasons: first, he had enjoyed use of the building for several years; second, the lead was replaced with Code 6 lead, which represented betterment and a longer life; and lastly, the architects would supervise without fee. (Note: the LDA stated that Code 4 should be sufficient for small areas in such localities and, therefore, exempted the architects: but cautious local knowledge suggested the upgrade in the new work.)

Lessons

* The critical issue is the specification by reference to a code, and the architects' failure to satisfy themselves that the code had been properly carried out. Do they have such a liability or, if specification is by reference, does that liability not pass to the contractor? In this case, the matter was palpable and should have been spotted by reasonable visual inspection.
* The further issue is the implication that the undertaking of this specific work could, retrospectively, be construed as a sufficient relevant event requiring a specific inspection by the architects. The problem with relevant events is that, generally, they become identified only retrospectively, by the law, in the event of failure.
* If the architects cannot be on site all the time, they clearly must judge, in advance, those parts of a building project deserving particular attention during construction.

LOOPY

Plumbing failed to conform to the relevant British Standard

The situation

Boilers began bursting in a block of 37 flats. Well, not exactly bursting, but splitting at the seams after the failure of thermostats. Three cylinders split and more threatened.

The problem investigated (1)

Two sets of expert witnesses were involved. Initially the problem was attributed to the fact that the working head (distance from cistern to cylinder) was greater than the grade of cylinder could cope with particularly at ground floor. But the experts then discovered a comprehensively bad job:

(i)   the 'open vents' from the cylinders did not go straight up, but looped causing airlock possibilities;
(ii)   cold-water distribution pipes also looped;
(iii) the open vents were insufficiently close-fitting into the cistern;
(iv)   there was insufficient pipe insulation in the unheated roof space;
(v)   there was insufficient cistern insulation in the unheated roof space.
       (Note: the experts disagreed as to whether any of the above had caused the problem)

The architects' position (1)

The architects had recommended the appointment of a services engineer, but Scottish Homes had refused to fund one. Problems with venting pipes, working heads, cold pipes and cistern insulation could be attributed to the contractor/sub-contractor. The architects had not specified the grade of cylinder since they could reasonably expect any competent plumber to be aware of the regulations. The architects were, in the above matters, able to rely upon the sub-contractor's knowledge and experience. The client accepted that. It raises, however, a slight question about inspection if none of the problems – not even the lack of insulation in the roof space – was spotted.

The problem (2)

The experts also discovered that the same pipe feeding from the roof cistern to the hot-water cylinder had a sub branch drawing off to feed the WC and wash-hand basin in the bathroom. BS 6700 requires that the cold-water feed to bathroom and WC should be taken from a dedicated cold-water supply to prevent possible back-flow. The installation was therefore in contravention.

The architects' position (2)

The installation had been discussed with the regional water authority which had raised no objections.

Outcome

The cost was met by each party paying approximately one-third: the architects, since their design did not comply with BS 6700; the contractor for reasons of the sub-contractor's incompetence; and the client by reason of betterment, in that they would end up with better hot-water cylinders.

Lessons

*   Perhaps the specification and installation did not receive sufficient attention and scrutiny by the architects; and perhaps an informal clearance from the regional water authority offers insufficient protection in circumstances of dispute. But the first issue is whether the architects should have had any responsibility at all for the central-heating installation. Since the client had refused to fund a services engineer, should that blame not be the client's?
*   The second issue is the standing of British Standards. Scots' law (Hunter vs. Hanley, and subsequent cases including Wester Hailes) does not require the necessary following of British Standards or codes of practice. What it requires is that the architect demonstrates knowledge of them; and if he/she decides to depart from them, they do so knowingly and with justification, which will subsequently be supported by other experts/architects in court as having been a competent course to follow. The court would listen to the architect's assessment of the balance of risk to determine whether the departure from the code of practice was competent or otherwise.

WATER WATER EVERYWHERE, AND NOT A DROP TO DRINK

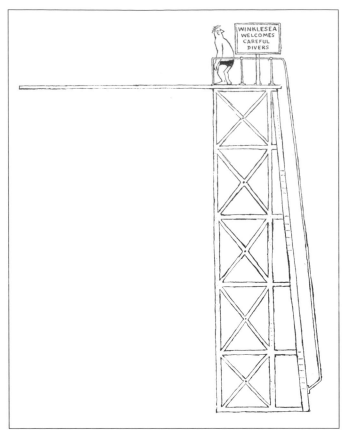

It is dangerous to presuppose use patterns

The situation

Teething troubles at a new swimming pool were uncovered during its first year of operation. Client relations were excellent (and the architect wished them to continue), and the pool was project-managed during briefing, construction and subsequent operation by a consultancy specialising in design and management of pools. The issue was the spread of water from the showers into the changing rooms, rendering them wet, slippy and dangerous, as one unfortunate swimmer had discovered painfully.

The contract

The original brief, for a simple cheap building with a traditional structure, was expanded when more money become available, only to be cut back again and then, at the very last moment, to have certain items reinstated. Order, counter-order, potential disorder. There were three clients – the local users, the local (distant) authority, and the project manager. The time scale varied from fast to stop, then to accelerate, with no time to think through the necessary changes. It is remarkable that so little did indeed go wrong.

The condition

Before cuts, the changing rooms were to have been entirely floored in non-slip tiles, with gulleys, soakaways etc. In savings, they had been cut since the anticipated water in the changing rooms could have been tackled by duckboards etc. At the last minute strips of non-slip had been reinstated in areas between the benches. The architect argued that the expert pool project manager had approved all the detailed decisions and had not insisted upon any changes during construction. He was entitled to rely upon that.

But the natural water in the changing rooms was exacerbated by unforeseen overspray from the showers, and it collected. Furthermore, it transpired that the location and benches and partitions had been set other than as instructed, and covered or obscured some of the non-slip tiles, revealing the slippy ones. The result was a painful injury and the risk of more.

Action

Skirts added to the shower cubicles remedied the problem in the changing room, but diverted the overspray to the toilets where it puddled. So the entire works involved nonslip tiles throughout (the cost of a specialist tiler from Glasgow), floor gulleys, channels and shower screens. It was not cheap.

Liability

Ultimately, the architect contributed one third: and the reasons were thus: first, as a result of all the works, the client got betterment; second, the client's expert project manager should share the responsibility of knowledge that it was not inherently safe enough. Third, the architect was liable for two reasons: failure to contain the overspray from the showers or to anticipate the effect it would have on other areas; and second, non-compliance with the Health and Safety document 'Safety in Swimming Pools' which states *'floor surfaces to wet circulation routes should not be slippery'*: or, in the circumstances of cuts, drawing this clause to the specific attention of the client.

Lessons

* Be aware of all relevant documentation and ensure your client takes responsibility if deviations are required for cost-cutting or other reasons.
* You cannot predict use patterns. Swimmers will move benches, operators screens, perhaps exposing a vulnerability in specification
* Triple headed clients in a commission whose budget is rapidly fluctuating should be avoided if possible. It is essential that the responsibility track is clear.

Moral

Water and moisture enjoy disproportionate stature in PI claims. They obey their own rules which humble mortals might best observe.

GUDDLE

Inadequacy of a timber means of escape

The situation

The client delays paying fees on a project to convert offices back into flats. When pursued, he counterclaims on the grounds that the property contained fewer flats than originally planned at the time of purchase, once building control had required substantial amendment. The original scheme had contained a timber fire escape which proved unacceptable. The client initiated arbitration proceedings, and the architect submitted evidence to the arbitration before informing the insurer.

The architect's case

The architect had worked for the client several times before, and they were friends. The developer was or should have been well aware of the risks and technical requirements of such conversions. In any case, the appointment had been for the limited service of initial concept sketches for a lump sum, to identify the number of flats that might be possible: but that would always have been susceptible to modification with planning and building control. The architect was never made aware of the client's budget or cost plan, or the assumptions the client was making in costing the development. The architect did not accept, therefore, that the client should have founded to the extent he did upon the drawings; and denied that the client had been informed there would be no additional costs. In such complicated inner city conversions, such an undertaking would have been impossible.

In any case, the architect had undertaken such work before, and was reasonably sure that building control would allow a relaxation.

The issue

Once drawings were submitted to building control, a relaxation was refused, and a redesign was required which resulted in smaller, fewer flats, and alterations to part of the roof to incorporate a new escape stair.

Cause of the problem

Very little regarding the architect's appointment was in writing, and the case that the preliminary plans were only for outline feasibility was not proved. Secondly, it was quite clear that the architect had noted the problem of the timber stair, but had assumed that the plan would be acceptable, as it had been in the past, and therefore had not warned the client. By that failure to warn, the architect had led the client into expense. Worse, by the submission to the arbitration process, he had compromised his insurance and came near to voiding it. The conclusion was an agreement by both parties not to pursue, and the architect received his fees (less the excess and an additional penalty for compromising the policy) from the insurance company.

Lessons

* To what extent are developers expected themselves to be expert, or should they all be treated as amateur?
* What constitutes a drawings-only service? How is it defined?
* The crippling lack of appointment documentation must be avoided.
* The architect must clearly inform his client when making critical assumptions, particularly those on which financial decisions are being made.

Moral

Too many assumptions lose money.

VALUELESS

The situation

The architect, in a grave financial position, seeks to recover substantial fees on an aborted scheme for a local authority, the figure based on the last contractor's estimate. The client notifies the intention to countersue for return of all fees on the project, on the grounds that the scheme aborted through the architect's financial incompetence, and that the work done was therefore, valueless. During the process, the architect went into liquidation, and the liquidators determined to press the suit in such a way that the client hardened his attitude, and the case went to law. However, they saw their duty as the pursuit of outstanding fees rather than defending the counterclaim which reached a critical state. The sum in question is over half a million pounds including the total fees and internal project costs.

The issue

The project for a major civic building had developed over some six years, with the architect providing an initial feasibility study, and then becoming more involved as the scheme deepened and developed. The client was initially uncertain over all items: the site, the components of the scheme, the budget, and the consultancy team pattern. The architect had offered a lead consultancy pattern, but the client had never responded. A year later, the council is still considering the above, without any appointment save to the architect. Three years in, the timescale is getting tight, and the architect is still pointing out that there is only an elemental cost, and quantity surveyors still have to be appointed. The site and brief are now fixed, but the council seeks the appointment of local quantity surveyors rather than those suggested by the architect. The estimates are now 25% higher than in year one. In October, the architect is permitted to appoint a QS, and reports that the elemental cost has risen by a further 30%, as a result of the changing brief. A year later, tenders were received at 150% higher than the original budget, and the appointment was terminated.

The architect's case

The architect had pressed the council repeatedly for the appointment of a QS, which had been done too late. The council had never accepted their offer of lead consultant. At no time had the client ever indicated a maximum upper limit budget, and the client had perpetually insisted upon increasing the specification following discussions with the Scottish Sports Council.

The loss adjuster

Initially, it was held that the architect had little or no case to answer. But as court proceedings fell under way, further facts came to light. First, the council was apparently assuming that the architect was acting as lead consultant until the appointment of a QS. Second, that, informally, a quantity surveyor had been working with the team prior to the separate appointment. Third, that the QS had reported higher costs of the project to the architect than the architect had been prepared to report to the client. It is clear that the architect hoped to make significant cost reductions which were foiled by the changes required by the Sports Council etc. The architect had, therefore, failed in his contractual duty to keep the client informed of the likely costs. The reserve duly increased to two thirds of the sum claimed.

The client reaches for his wallet – or is it his sword?

Result

The claim was settled at 10% of the claim plus expenses (about the same).

Lessons

* The client should have been compelled to clarify the appointment much earlier on.
* The architect should have identified the cause of the various cost increases and reported them to the client as they occurred, prior to the client committing himself to site purchase etc.

Moral

You cannot commit or spend the client's money without his/her prior authority.

OVERSIGHT NOT OVERLOOKED

The situation

A hawk-eyed planning officer spots the eruption of new lift-housing on the front roof of a seven-storeyed Edwardian warehouse being converted to speculative offices. He does not like it. For a start, the building is listed and the lift-housing lacks planning permission. He enforces, the contract is halted and the fun begins.

The fun

The architect advises the client there is no value in going to appeal. The planners would never accept the lift-housing. So, in mid contract, Otis is wheeled in to devise a new, ground-based lift system and remove (and attempt to salvage what they can from) the redundant one. The client has to accept less lettable floorspace at ground floor, and the contractor has to demolish the new lift-housing and make good the damage caused to the finished builder work. Client is eventually seeking £140K+.

The cause

This was one of those cases which the architect could hardly deny. His view was sought in public at a site meeting, in circumstances which made it almost impossible for the architect to deny liability as the insurers expected him to. There were two causes to the error. First, at the point of planning permission (stage D), the client had not yet made up his mind about the second (front) lift shaft, even though there had been an old one in that location. So the drawings submitted showed the existing lift shaft only. That defence has its peculiarities. The building was listed and the permission given should have been in detail. Thus all parties, including the planning officials, shared some liability. The second cause was that, by the time a decision had been taken, well into stage F, those in charge of the project forgot to check the original planning permission drawings; and remained blissfully ignorant of the fact that the new lift-housing they were proposing for the building's façade had never been floated in front of the planners. Given the architect's instant realisation that the housing was indeed a carbuncle upon the façade, it is curious that such perceptions did not occur earlier. There cannot have been any check between building warrant and planning permission drawings. The loss assessor believed it an oversight.

Implications

It is arguable that the lift would always have had to be on the ground floor, so the loss of utility and the more expensive equipment for that system would always have been at the client's expense. The liability attaching to the architect was for, effectively, the costs of constructing and then removing a redundant lift system, and for the delays resulting from the affair.

Result

The architect was liable for the additional costs of the new system. However, assessment of the consequential loss did not follow a straight track. It transpired that, because the client owned the contractor, there was no formal contract the architect had seen; and, therefore, formal provision neither for a contract completion date nor for L & A damages. Furthermore, the contract sum was already greatly exceeded and the programme running behind. Nonetheless, the insurer made a best guess at the real consequential loss (approximately one third that sued for) and paid into court. Settlement was achieved at slightly less than that (thus exempting the insurer from costs).

A more discreet form of lift housing

Lessons

* Do not leave important decisions relating to a listed building till after planning permission. It could negate an entire development.
* Ensure that the developed and detailed plans into E & F, and the contract drawings at G, conform to planning permission.

Moral

The later you allow a client to make decisions, the more expensive the result is likely to be.

CONFLICT OF INTEREST

The workmanship was less than satisfactory

The situation

The client notifies a claim on the grounds of late completion of a holiday house from which he required income. The architect being in liquidation, the files do not seem to have been available to clarify the background.

The issue

The job involved interior modifications and an extension, and the contract was for a two-month period. It was then extended by another month (50%), then by two, three, and eventually eight months. By the time the contract was determined, the building inspector found a number of substantial defects which required the appointment of another architect for a survey and report. The new architect met the original on site to agree the works to be done.

The defects

Generally, they were of appalling but palpable bad workmanship: plaster-work requiring redone, ditto timber-work damaged or wrongly installed, loose tiles, wrong insulation, wrong windows (single glazed rather than the specified double glazed) damaged and structurally inadequate roof structure, etc. ad infinitum. The clients had frequently flagged their concern about the architect's lack of presence on site and defects appeared to support them. Yet most of the work had been certified by the architect.

Ethics

Worse, the building contractor was the architect himself. The architect claimed that he had, as required, informed the client of his involvement in the firm and how, during the contract, he would cease to be an architect in favour of being the builder. No such letter was found and the clients pleaded the contrary in court, that it was only after work began on site that they became aware of the double interest.

Furthermore, only one month after the architect (in whatever capacity) had accepted liability for the defects, his building company went into liquidation before carrying out the works.

Worse, at the point of completing his PI form, the architect had answered *'No'* to the question about any interest in or association with any other practice, company or organisation: and had not notified the insurer of any change.

Consequences

The architect had no cover whatsoever in his capacity as a builder: and his failure to declare his other interest to the insurer put his insurance at risk and his membership of the professional organisations in immediate danger. However, the insurance company held it possible that the architect's failings *as architect* in certifying clearly bad work would lay the insurers open to enforcement rights under the 1930 Insurers Act, and therefore accepted liability to cover the damages for that aspect. The claim was finally settled for rather less than that claimed.

Implications

The professional codes are clear about the necessity to communicate to all relevant parties any actions undertaken by the architect that might impinge on his independence of judgement, and to clarify and resolve any potential conflict of interest. This disgraceful case is not unique in Scotland.

It raises, however, the matter of how difficult it is for an architect to prove independence of judgement on a contract if he has a financial interest in one of the other parties (contractor, sub-contractor, client, tenant, supplier, etc). It might perhaps be done by the Caesar's wife syndrome i.e. be unnecessarily harsh to demonstrate objectivity. A certifying architect will never be able to enjoy credible independence of judgement if he claims to be acting as an independent consulting architect on the same site as a construction or supply company in which he has a financial interest.

A clean break is required: the architect should have relinquished his role as an architect, invited the client to appoint another, informed his PI company and settled down to building well. The pretence of certifying yourself is not what professionalism embraces.

Lesson

Make absolute distinctions between your role as an independent consulting architect and any other you undertake, and ensure that all relevant parties are informed in writing.

Moral

If you wear several hats, don't let one slip over your eyes.

BOTCH UP

Failure to spot the contractor's deviations on site

The situation

Failure of eight windows in a house extension leading to water ingress, damp and consequent problems.

The architect's position

The problems are those of the contractor for which the architect instructs remedy (but does not check that it is carried out). It is not. Nor does the architect notify his insurer. Worse, believing the problem to be minor, he assures the client that he (architect) will cover any costs of remedy (believing it to be in the hundreds of pounds. Out by a factor of 20).

Three years later

The builder is in liquidation: the client commissions an expert report pending suing the architect.

The expert witness report

The report concludes the architect's specification was rather unspecific (e.g. match existing dimensions). Since the windows that arrived on site were too large, the builder could not use the specified precast cills and, instead, cast new ones *in situ* using the dpc as shuttering. The architect's original detail was poor, but the as-built detail with the new cast cills was dreadful, and the cills themselves were uneven, with a fall inwards puddling up against the wood. The windows to judge by their rotten state had not been adequately treated or prepared. Poor cills and a poor detail provided a convenient path for water to enter the house.

The insurer's response

The loss adjuster advised the insurers to repudiate the claim on the grounds of failure to notify, and on the undertaking to cover the costs of remedy. The insurers withdrew cover and support. The architect protested on the grounds that since the problem was perceived as being the builder's, there were no circumstances to be notified. Ah! In that case, why had he offered to cover any costs? However, the insurers relented. The decision was taken at MD level to restore cover possibly because of the insured's high excess being reasonably close to the likely financial out-turn.

Liability

Liability attached to the architect because the work had been certified, *'which would constitute an acknowledgement that the insured was satisfied ... that the windows were satisfactory'* and the amount of retention amounted to barely 0.5% of the actual cost. Whereas there might not have been liability attaching to the architect in spotting that the windows were too large, or might not have been adequately treated, reasonable visual inspection should have picked up on the cills and the as-built detail; and remedial action could have taken place much earlier and much more cheaply.

Lessons

* Beware of failure to spot contractor deviations on site, with the architect having to pay for it.
* When problems arise, do not assume too easily that it is contractor responsibility. Investigate thoroughly and rapidly, prior to taking up a position.

THE DELEGATOR

Overture

The curtain rises on this tragic operetta when a bass drum roll announces the arrival of an unexpected writ for *c.*£100K jointly against the *architetto* and a *contractore* for which there had been no forewarning. We never see the *contractore* who, first, has moved to Middle England, thence to liquidation.

Act One

The client makes the case in a brusque basso profundo. The stone outer skin of the building had faults: why, you could take out entire blocks of stone. They were not fixed, they were not mortared, they were not tied and the copes were loose. They had had to take action, remedy the work and now sought payment. The insurer's notary, in a dashing aria, denies any liability and triumphantly questions the validity of the entire suit. Where is the proof of any wrongdoing by the architect? Enter the architect with a reprise: *'No! No! e la responsibilità del contractore!'* The client withdraws. Curtain.

Act Two

The curtain rises upon the client entering with his 'very expensive' advisor (or expert witness). In a duet, that soon becomes a monologue in recitative, new details of the case are laid out: steel dowels to fix the copes were lacking, wall ties were various, inadequate in number and placing, joints were random, drawings were unspecific and the mortar was too weak. They plunge down a thicker writ, and leave. Enter the notary, gravely, accompanied by the former job architect and assistant. He asks them to describe the contract. In a melancholy duo, they describe the documentation, the job and the inspections which an increasingly agitated notary joins in a trio to question whether site visits were thorough enough. At the point the job architect states that the specification had been left to the quantity surveyor, he interrupts furiously with the famous aria: *'Questo e la responsibilità del architetto!'*, and stalks out. Curtain.

Act Three

In this short act, the notary examines the issues and is soon joined by the ghostly, tall, cadaverous vision of the expert witness who rises, Salieri-style, to counterpoint the notary in establishing the minimum detail an architect is required to give the contractor. Although good practice, delineation of all mortar joints was not essential. Although a level of skill can be expected of both the contractor and the specialist stone sub-contractor, responsibility for specification could not be passed either to them (mortar strength) or to the QSS (location, frequency and type of wall ties). Furthermore, the absence of at least some of the wall ties should have been spotted by reasonable visual inspection; given their role in the essential structure of the building. He concludes gloomily, in harmonic duet with the expert witness, that liability has been established.

La mura è mobile ...

Finale

Enter the notary, briskly, red hair glowing, teeth ready for action. He has paid 25% into court and sets out upon his favourite occupation: reducing the settlement. The operetta suffers from the absence of the client/notary duet; although echoes and vestiges can be heard through the window, the melancholy basso profundo of the claim being overwhelmed by staccato interjections by the notary: *'be reasonable! be wise! cut your losses! finish now! look to the future!'* finishing on a triumphant high note: *e vero, e finito!*

Lessons

* Responsibility for specification lies with the architect.
* Given the structural nature of wall ties, some inspection of them is essential.
* The architect's normal responsibilities do not diminish, however expert or specialist the contractor.

PAPERCHASE

No record of the many meetings with the client

A sad little case

What went wrong with this tiny project was never in dispute. There were defects in a tiny cottage which the purchaser's surveyor did not spot. The architect was employed to specify the works required for a local authority grant (with some minor additions) whilst the surveyor was sued. The client's resources stretched to the grant sum only.

The writ

The arrival of a writ was unexpected, irritating the architect. It alleged failings arising from changes between specification and contract: the solum was gravel rather than compact sand and concrete as specified; the stair repairs were in white wood rather than redwood to match; windows were single-glazed casement instead of double-glazed pivot; the slates were broken and loose, infilled with cement and without sarking and so on. The case against the builder was evident; the case against the architect that he had made only four brief visits in a four-month contract and had not spotted what was afoot.

The next step

Both architect and builder claimed that at many meetings with the client, the specification had been reduced at her request as a result of lack of funds and that everything complained of was as per agreement. That they were causing problems of damp and water penetration they had no knowledge of, since they were not allowed access.

Complications

Many. That is the interest of the case. The client was on Legal Aid, and the sum sued for was under £10K. It would cost more to defend than to pay. The builder went into liquidation, and was represented by Legal Aid also. The architect was likely to face the entire amount under joint and several liability. Second, the architect, whose excess (or self-assured sum) would clearly be required, was unlikely to agree to contribute it without, at least, pressure from an external expert witness. What was discovered was a lack of paper. It seemed that the architect might have issued a final certificate but it could not be found. If he had, the liability was his. Nothing could be proved. As for the discussions about changing the specification with the client, the sheriff had much to say (even if the insurer's lawyer disagreed vehemently): *'I would have expected {the architect} to have taken notes in accordance with good professional practice at such meetings . . . Both defenders aver in their pleadings that the terms of the specification were varied As there are no written communications . . . it must be presumed these communications were verbal.'* No records to defend himself, no final certificate, the architect is being marched to the clothes-line, the pegs being got ready. The lawyer tried again, by attacking lack of specification of the architect's duty in the writ, namely what had the client contracted him to do? on the grounds that a defender cannot be found to be liable on grounds not specified by the pursuer. The sheriff dissented: there was a sufficiency of averrments, he thought, *'to enable the court to imply duties there would seem to be'.*

Settlement

The case was settled immediately prior to a full trial for c.60% of the sum claimed, shared equally between architect and builder. Costs of expert witness, court fees, lawyers etc. came to rather more.

Lesson

If you don't listen to Practice Information or the Practice Guide, be aware that the sheriff does, and the yardstick by which you will be assessed is *'good professional practice'.*

SPEND, SPEND, SPEND

*When the client instructed additional items,
he knew he would be increasing the cost*

The setting

We are in court: well, not exactly, but studying a closed record adjusted and amended all with consequent delay over the previous five years. Trial is imminent for a sum just under £300K (+ *c*.£150K interest), itself reduced from the original £400K (+ interest). Hmmm.

The cause

The client alleged that the costs of the conversion and enhancement of a workaday building into a sophisticated house outreached his original budget by slightly over 50%. The architects had clearly not followed the contractual clauses in the Architect's Appointment (i.e. informing the client if either contract period or sum were to be materially varied). They had not shown sufficient skill and care, and were therefore liable. Cost overrun was admitted. But was the responsibility as simple as that? Please remember that the case was settled out of court and some of the issues were never legally tested.

Client issues

The client admitted that speed of conversion had been a primary objective and that he had approved accelerated patterns e.g. a prime cost contract and no bills of quantities, in order to achieve that. Architect and QS held that they understood that time was more important than cost: but nothing in writing sustained that. Haste governed the contract. Some wonderful additions and an admirable heightening in the quality of materials and workmanship were instructed during the last nine months of the contract, following a cost report which indicated some money still to spare. The client maintained that had he been aware of the real costs at that date, he would not have instructed these changes which made up the majority of the claim. Quantifying the extent of damages, calculated like this, was one of the reasons for delay in process. The consultants had spent money which he did not have without his authority. He alleged that a primary reason why he had not received accurate cost information upon which to base his decisions was late production of information by the architect to the QS: of 243 drawings, 18% were submitted to the QS first; 48% to QS and builder at the same time; 22% to builder before the QS; and 12% not to the QS at all. The latter did not have the information to cost: ergo, the architect was liable. In any case, if the QS cost estimate was so far out, an architect of reasonable skill and care should have been able to spot that and address the problem.

Architect issues

The architects' defence was fourfold – one substantive. First, the atmosphere of rush which would inevitably increase the possibility of risk. Second, that, although the QS might not have had drawings, he had been issued with sufficiently full, dated AIs upon which to make his calculations. Third, the client had such a personal interest in the project that they were entitled to believe that when he instructed additional items, he was knowingly increasing the contract value. The substantive defence was to bring in the QS as third party. During the final nine months, with an acceleration of expensive, high-quality finishing work, QS cost control collapsed. The cost report at the start was substantially ill founded, in that it undervalued work, had not included for AIs or for increases to labour costs. There was nothing for the next nine months until a retrospective report, when it was too late to alter anything. The QS had been separately appointed and had the duty to report to the client on cost progress not the architect.

QS issues

The QS maintained he had done a professional job hampered by late production of information and client urgency.

Settlement

The case was settled at 25% of its total potential liability with a 40% contribution from the QS, plus 33% oncost for expert witnesses, court and professional fees.

Underlying issues

An excellent settlement (implying attrition rather than justice) to a worrying case. The court might well have held that the architect should have demanded very frequent cost reports during a period of high expenditure. Otherwise, he would not have been able to fulfil his duty according to the Architect's Appointment irrespective of the contractual position of the QS. The court would also have considered whether the final building was, as the defenders claimed, value for money, thereby denying the concept of loss. The client intended the house for his family and, therefore, did not regard it as a commodity for potential sale; and, as a consequence, pled that even if the house was value for money, he had been denied the opportunity to make savings or possibly to spend the money elsewhere.

Lesson

A difficult time-constrained contract with high client input required greater rather than lesser monitoring of cost.

Moral

When the costings of a project appear too good to be true, cross-examine the truth.

OLD HAT

A problem with doors

The situation

Six external doors being fitted to an historic building undergoing renovation and conversion failed even before the subcontract was complete. They were warping and jamming to a degree far greater than appropriate, adding to the architect's other irritations with the joiner-work. They were, claimed the client, deteriorating and unsuitable for their purpose.

The case

The doors had been specified as redwood, to BS 1186 'Quality of Timber and Workmanship in Joinery'. The (domestic) sub-contractor claimed that an acceptable standard could not be achieved using redwood, and that the problems were those of the specifier. Even the architect seemed minded to agree, notifying the insurers that *'there may be some doubt about the applicability of the standard'* in the exposed circumstances of large external doors.

Coup de grace

Indeed there was. Not long afterwards, the architect notified the insurer that BS 1186 had been superseded by BS 4978 which advised against redwood doors in such locations. This, the loss adjuster accepted that even though BS 4978 was not the most appropriate one either.

The contract gets murkier

In the meantime, the contract was coming to an end. The architect had instructed the remaking of the doors at the contractor's expense. The sub-contractor had informed the main contractor that he repudiated all liability for the cost and would sue the main contractor for restitution in full. If he did, the main contractor would sue the client. The loss adjuster advised settlement, since the contractor's alleged workmanship defects had no bearing on the door problem, and the retention was therefore not available to pay for it.

Settlement

An excellent price for new doors was obtained which, with the architect's excess being brought in, led to a settlement at less than 50% of the estimated liability.

General considerations

Whether or not the old BS had still been in force, those doors would still have failed in that location (which raises, as the late Arthur Wright PPRIAS used to point out, the issue of whether the BSI would ever have accepted any responsibility for their standards). But how come neither the contractor, nor the expert sub-contractor spotted the inaccurate specification? And if it was quite so obvious that redwood was inappropriate in that function, did no liability or responsibility attach to the specialist sub-contractor for making and supplying without query?

Moral

Use outdated standards at your peril.

DOWNHILL ALL THE WAY

The situation

Two claims are lodged by a house developer for failure in house-layout plans leading to reworking, re-excavation and loss of development value totalling the best part of a seven-figure sum.

The circumstance

It is a sad commentary on the current status of architects that the commission had nothing to do with the house design; that was reserved for the in-house 'designers'. The architect's three-dimensional skill and training was reserved for site layout, sewers and roads; a clever man might cram houses in, but is not allowed to design them. Both sites were large, to contain phased development, and both were on slopes one more severe than the other. The architect had obtained subcontract site-survey information from an engineer.

The event

On the first site, complete site works were undertaken and the majority of the site developed but, when it came to the erection of the final group of houses, a site-survey error in terms both of the site boundary and of levels was identified. The remedy required, inter alia, the reworking of the access roads, services and sewers. The larger, two-phase site was on a much steeper slope with access problems to the village; the local authority sought a different access to that proposed by the architect.

The commission

The commission for the second site included the determination of site levels, roadways, driveway gradients, sewers, planning permission and construction consent. The council had disagreed with the architect's original access and proposed a feed of an existing route, for which revised drawings were prepared. Immediately after planning permission had been received, the builder began construction, the architect assuring him that construction consent would be forthcoming. Well, application for such consent was not prompt and the site was over four months into development when construction consent was refused on the grounds of too steep a gradient in the roadway. The client also discovered errors in site boundaries.

The consequence

The consequences were hugely expensive. The client had to re-dig roads and sewers; the new layouts required unforeseen retaining walls and a house plot was forfeited for a new sewer route. All houses required redesigning and, for reasons of levels, phase II became impossible.

Settlement

It was always possible that, once the council had restricted access, phase II was going to be undevelopable. Furthermore, whatever the architect said, by beginning on site prior to construction consent, the housebuilder had run the risk of the work being abortive. At no time had the architect instructed preempting construction consent, although his assurance that it would be automatic was horribly unwise and, in the event, inaccurate. The case was settled out of court for about one seventh of the original and one half of the amended claim.

A problem with access, site boundary and levels

Lessons

* Perhaps a contributory factor might have been a failure to correlate the original information properly with the implications of the change in road access following council intervention. Always check that knock-on consequences of design changes are followed through.
* The expense was at least partly attributable to the fact that the errors were only discovered once substantial construction work had begun.
* Site layouts for house builders do not represent the pinnacle of design challenge for an architect. They help pay bills, but are otherwise humdrum events until, that is, errors in setting out and levels are made. Thereafter, they are far from humdrum.

Moral

There are usually teeth behind a yawn.